# The Death of Public Schools

## INGRID LAOS

Copyright © 2020 Ingrid Laos

All rights reserved.

ISBN-13:978-1-7344961-0-9

## IN HONOR OF

My Father

> Give me your tired, your poor,
> Your huddled masses yearning to breathe free,
> The wretched refuse of your teeming shore.
> Send these, the homeless, tempest-tost to me,
> I lift my lamp beside the golden door!"

**Emma Lazarus (November 2, 1883)**
The New Colossus

This poem is a cornerstone of American history. A statement about the foundation of our country. A country that has opened its doors to generation after generation of immigrants. We remember images in history books of poor and hungry Irish, Polish, and Italian families coming in from the cold with their dark grey or black weathered coats. It was barely enough to brace the chill North Atlantic air. Their tired faces and fear-laden eyes; fear that they would be rejected, fear that they would be sent back into a tempestuous ocean. And, yet, Lady Liberty stands tall and majestic. She is a lighthouse of freedom and opportunity. She is a symbol of this country —of the freedom and opportunity that is bound to meet you, as many believe.

We no longer see masses of immigrants arriving at our shores. We no longer see their faces. There is a grand sense of anonymity. Our first glimpse of them is when they arrive at school. We can identify the fear in their eyes, the anonymity, the lack of knowing the English language. We can even take a guess at what block they live on or where they work in our community. Teachers hold a torch now —a torch of freedom and opportunity. For if success is not for the immigrants, the immigrants are determined that it will be for their children. Whatever their children will learn at school will create a better future. A better future for all. The future of their children will outshine their sacrifice. At least that is the hope. Teachers are this era's torch-bearers; they stand tall like Lady Liberty.

## TABLE OF CONTENTS

| | | |
|---|---|---|
| I | Where We Begin | 1 |
| II | Let Me Tell You About Teachers | 15 |
| III | Bear With Me: It's Going To Get A Tad Heavy | 33 |
| IV | Hear Me Roar | 69 |
| V | Some Truths | 89 |
| VI | We Can Create Something New For Our Children | 105 |
| VII | In Gratitude | 137 |
| | Acknowledgements | 141 |

# DEDICATION

This book is dedicated to every teacher who has taught, is teaching, or will teach in America. This book is of them, by them, and for them. This book is for the heroes, the givers, the communitarians, the organizers, the achievers, the dreamers, the intellectuals, the workers, the humanitarians. This book is for you, the teachers.

INGRID LAOS

# INTRODUCTION

The intention of this book is to open up conversation, to stir up dialogue between teachers, parents, administration, and society at large. I wrote this book as a teacher, while teaching in the classroom, and for the purpose of addressing education and how it looks today from a teacher's standpoint.

Every year, we're asked to do more. Every single year. We're asked to work more with less. Fewer resources. Less pay. The list is endless: write highly detailed lesson plans per day per subject, grade nine assessments per subject per quarter, encourage attendance, give rewards for everything, come up with contests, monitor student progress, meet and appease parents, meet the demands of the administration, meet the demands of the District. Oh yeah...and teach.

We lose teachers at about the ten year mark, which means we're losing them just as they're becoming an expert in the field. The country is losing about 8% of teachers per year. That's a couple hundred thousand teachers per year. It's the sounding of an alarm that so many people are dropping out.

You need two things to be a teacher: you need to be extremely patient and you need to be a master of what you're teaching. It takes practice and experience to become a master. As for patience, you either have it or you don't. It's hard to foster. As a result, we already have a very select percentage of the population that has both of these qualities, and we're losing them at the rate of 8% per year. "New teachers remain in our profession an average of just 4.5 years."

How many people do you think can walk into a room of 20 elementary school children and keep them focused and on task for eight hours? Let me paint you a picture. While you're teaching your daily Math lesson, you'll need to get the phone because little Suzy is going home early, and your teacher neighbor really needs a bathroom break so please hit the pause button. In the meantime, little

Johnny is throwing pieces of an eraser at his classmates because he needs attention and you get to resolve that while simultaneously keeping an eye on your neighbor's classroom. And then you can continue teaching your Math lesson for the first time because you know you will re-teach it in small groups at least three more times. Don't forget that you'd better finish in that hour you've set aside because your grade level only has time for one math lesson per day. If your students didn't "get it," then that's on you because you can't afford to fall behind or you will not have taught everything for April's state test. You will have millions of requests, millions of arguments you'll have to solve, millions of fires that will need to be put out, with the many levels or layers of teaching you will need to do. Children that will get it the first time and other children that may not get it after the sixth time. Teachers are dropping like flies.

We've got to invest in our teachers if we want to keep them. The death of public schools will be due to the death of teachers. Without good teachers at the helm, the cause is lost. Teachers have lost heart. They are discouraged, they are tired, they are resigned. They are resigned about the possibility of change, the possibility of improvement, and the future of the profession. They are looking to "jump ship" or quit, rather than look for a solution because the solution seems impossible. Besides, it feels like no one is listening to this call for help. So, why even bother?

What can we work on to add value for teachers?
1) Fair compensation for the value they bring
2) Good administrative leaders that are humble, listen to their workers, and lead by example
3) Retirement/Benefits (Everybody wants this.)
4) Respect. This involves giving teachers more choices within the system, holding them up in acknowledgment as equally as we hold them up to their high moral standards, and listening to them. There is nothing worse than overriding a teacher's informed opinion, bypassing her/his opinion, or worse yet, not even asking.
5) Gratitude. While most teachers feel gratitude from at least someone in their community, teachers don't often feel gratitude or real appreciation from society at large.

I feel a sense of urgency in writing this book. We're living in a time where many citizens are waking up to harsh political and world realities. It's only logical that Americans also wake up to the realities of our education system, which is our only real future.

This book is a fight for teachers. It's a fight for them to feel valued. For their value to be recognized by teachers and non-teachers alike. Everyone yearns to feel valued in order to simply keep striving in life. Think about it. If you don't see value in something, would you do it? If you didn't value your car, would you buy it? If you didn't value your friendships, would you spend time with those people? If you didn't feel valued on the job, would you stay?

Teachers don't feel valued. Believe me when I tell you this. If teachers don't start to see value in their profession, then they will continue to drop out of it. I can't tell you how many times I've heard from long time teachers: "I love teaching. I love the kids. But it's just too hard. I can't make it in this system for 30 years...I need to jump into something else –I don't know what yet –but anything else and I have to get out NOW."

It's a "save yourself from this job" kind of mentality in teaching right now. We're more than burned out. We're sinking and we're sinking fast. Is this what we want? The future of education which means...the future of our children...which means the future of our world...is in the hands of women and men who feel like they aren't valued, and they're looking to get off the sinking ship (i.e., the broken education system) as quickly as possible. Think about it. Truly.

This is not an academic book because I don't just want academics to read it. This book is written in clear, concise terms and as jargon free as possible for the moms and dads who send their children to public schools. This book is a call for the public to rise and to say, "we can do this better." This book is for Americans to have access to facts and perspective in order to take action!

"Education is like Alice in Wonderland because everything is upside down, nothing makes sense, and you don't know how to get out."

-**Ms. Blanch**, veteran elementary teacher

# THE DEATH OF PUBLIC SCHOOLS

# PART I
# WHERE WE BEGIN

INGRID LAOS

# THE FRAMERS

If you've heard of the Framers at any point in U.S. history class, then you know that it was a special group of enlightened thinkers living in a fairly small area (square footage) of this young country, at one very significant time. Think big names like John Adams, Thomas Jefferson or Benjamin Franklin. They made history. They grabbed it with their zealous hands, they molded it as desired, and they threw it at America. They are the architects of one of the greatest representative democracies that has ever existed in civilization –America. Through endless discord, through hot summers, through opposing philosophies, the Framers pushed through, and somehow manifested documents that would dictate democracy in America and created ideals that Americans of the future would strive to reach.

What did the Framers think of education? What did they *do* for education? Well, part of the problem or not (your perspective will dictate) is that education wasn't mentioned in the actual Constitution of the United States. Education became one of the many unenumerated powers left to the states. Moreover, public education didn't really exist until the 19th century because children were educated at home by their mothers beforehand.[i] Education meant reading books at home; there was a presumption that every person would seek to educate oneself almost as a moral obligation. Did the Framers leave out education because they were short-sighted about how education would evolve in America? Hard to say, but generally speaking, the Framers weren't short-sighted. It seems that their silence when it came to certain topics was an intentional one.

Do we know what the Framers, at least, thought about education? Well, John Adams famously wrote that "there should not be a district of one mile square, without a school in it, not founded by a charitable individual, but maintained at the public expense of the people themselves," which is in clear support of public education.[ii]

Thomas Jefferson, drafter of the Declaration of Independence and founder of the first public university, was probably the most vocal about public education being necessary for the preservation of a democracy. Jefferson wrote in a letter, amongst many other letters, "I know no safe depositary of the ultimate powers of the society but the people themselves; and if we think them not enlightened enough to exercise their control with a wholesome discretion, the remedy is not to take it from them, but to inform their discretion by education. This is the true corrective of abuses of constitutional power." Benjamin Franklin, founder of the University of Pennsylvania, penned the quote, "If a man empties his purse into his head no man can take it from him. An investment in knowledge pays the best interest."[iii]

And so, the lack of enumeration in the Constitution doesn't mean that the Framers didn't think about education. Actually, it seems clear through their writing that they believed education to be a public duty. A public responsibility, if you will. That being said, it would have been hard for them to envision public education for a huge country of more than 300 million people. Regardless, the Framers had a very concrete understanding of the dangers an uneducated public could face. They knew what an oligarch meant and they had traveled far from that to avoid that destiny again.

Ah! But maybe the Framers needed to leave a bit more guidance on the matter. A bit more of a blueprint for the American public to carry on the expense of public education. I wonder if they saw public education today, would they nod in agreement with how it is structured? Or would they shake their heads in defeat?

# The Setup

If the Framers could be present today, would they be on board with how different the system works from one state to another? Would they accept the lack of true national leadership on education? Would they agree with *who* handles the school system's budget? Would they let Superintendents have such large districts to manage? And what would they have to say about the School Boards? Are School Boards serving their function and purpose with fidelity?

When you begin to peel back the curtain of our education system and the way it was set up, it becomes clear rather quickly that it's in a bit of a hazy fog. Early on in the 18th century, it was clear that education would fall under the umbrella of the 10th Amendment to the Constitution, which basically delegates powers to the states, when it isn't given to the federal government expressly. As you read about the history of the school system in America, the story begins as the local government's responsibility to educate the children of its community. As cities got larger, and transportation and communication got better, the state became more integrated.

Eventually, education agencies were created at the state level. As you read further, you come to understand that education has developed into a heavily intertwined local and state entity, with a smattering of national influence, and each entity across the nation seems to take on its own shape.[iv]

*The State*

The state's role in education began primarily through money. It started by supporting growing local communities and allocating money to the public schools through the state taxation system. The system works on the premise that, if it was the state taxpayers who paid for the schools, they should be the ones who direct how that money is used.[v] As time went on, the state could assert some control and uphold requirements for an "equality" within schools by giving money to those schools that were following these checks in place. Eventually, states created education agencies, which was basically a greater workforce, to manage the money and requirements that the state placed upon the schools.

Each state's constitution does require it to provide a school system where children may receive an education. Many state constitutions also contain express provisions for creating educational curricula. Some constitutions empower state authorities to choose textbooks and educational materials. State governments also have the power to legislate for education, or they can authorize officials to establish, select, and regulate curriculum. Finally, state legislatures can set mandatory requirements for students to graduate.[vi]

*Local*

This is where it all began. Back in 1779, Thomas Jefferson introduced a proposal in the Virginia Assembly that the citizens of each county would elect three aldermen who would have general charge of the schools.[vii] The local communities would raise money for education and, eventually, elect, hire, or appoint people to run the schools. These local bodies, or school districts, decide exactly how schools will operate. Each school district is governed by a School Board, whose members are either elected by the public or appointed. Nationally, 96% of school boards are elected by a popular vote. Local school boards are also responsible for establishing curricula, hiring personnel, and deciding when schools should be closed, consolidated, or constructed. Local school boards are in charge of raising about half of government school funding. They do this by collecting property taxes on all of the homes and businesses within their district or by allowing the city council to do so on their behalf. Finally, each school board also appoints a Superintendent, typically an experienced school administrator to oversee all the schools in their district.[viii]

*The Superintendent*

The position of Superintendent was created about a decade after the creation of public schools. It was created by the local boards, without any statutory authority, in order for a professional hire to take over growing demands of the school system. A community may look like a district, a county or a city, and, as communities grew, so did the demands of overseeing the school system.[ix] Thus, the position of Superintendent came to be. The Superintendent is regarded as the CEO of the school community.

What are the requirements of a Superintendent? In general, a Superintendent must have a teaching certificate, at least a few years of teaching experience, a master's degree or higher, and 2-5 years of administrative experience as a principal or other school administrator. The qualifications for a Superintendent are set by each school district, and therefore, the details will differ from place to place. In addition, some states will require a certificate in leadership or the passage of specific exams.

What does a Superintendent do? The Superintendent is a contractual worker for a specific length of time. Actual duties may include: the hiring and placement of principals for the district, hiring for positions within the board of education, making decisions about educational programs, spending, and staffing for particular facilities. The Superintendent has control over principals and is supposed to visit the schools in the community to ensure their working order. He or she should be familiar with each school in the district to ensure that the necessary qualifications for the actual building and staff are being met. The Superintendent is also supposed to steer the district's policies and mission in a progressive manner toward excellence for present-day students.[x]

The "Superintendency" has evolved through three major periods in its short history. The first period began shortly after the creation of public schools in the early 1800's and extends to the early part of the 20th century. The first state Superintendent was appointed in 1812 in New York. The main function of these early Superintendents was to handle the accounting activities of state education funds and data collection. The Superintendent of that period had little influence on educational issues.[xi]

The "professional Superintendent" period covers the first half of the 20th century into the 1960s. In this phase, the Superintendent's influence grew tremendously. School districts became big businesses within their local communities. They hired hundreds or thousands of employees (depending on location) and spent millions of tax dollars. During this phase, Superintendents made most of the major decisions affecting districts and were usually supported by the local boards. They were seen as civic leaders of the local community and wielded immense power over the daily life of the school system. Disagreements between the Superintendent and the School Boards were rare, as the Superintendent received much support.[xii]

The "modern Superintendency" picks up after the 1960s and carries us through the present-day. This period can be described as clouded and uncertain. In the 1960s, the federal government stepped into education like never before, adding new demands to the system. The civil rights movement, antiwar movement, increased immigration, and the teacher union movement created an environment where there was much greater involvement and scrutiny from the public towards education. School leaders, including the Superintendent, were no longer trusted to conduct the affairs of the schools without considerable observation and criticism. In order to be successful, the Superintendent of today must be proficient in politics and the art of persuasion. The job has shifted from overseeing and managing to creating and maintaining relationships, and navigating the uncertainty of the future with skill and finesse.[xiii]

*Federal Law*

Federal law really stepped into the mix of education in the 20th century. It's been through the exercise of federal law that we've seen the education system adapt to the changing tides of America. Due to federal law, we've experienced racial desegregation of schools, we've seen children with disabilities be brought into mainstream schools for an equal education, and we've seen swarms of immigrants be welcomed into the system. While this evolution of our country and our system has been well-intentioned and adaptive, it's undeniable that it has also brought about serious, new demands on school systems. For example, teaching children with disabilities requires different skillsets and training for teachers and administrators. And, with the immigrant population, many of these immigrants come with little to no formal education from their home countries. Generally speaking, these new expectations haven't been met with the adequate attention or training necessary and has caused serious problems.[xiv]

Surprisingly, the federal government is in charge of less than 10 percent of all school funding. Its funding is targeted to help students most in need of extra support, such as Title I funding for low-income families, and IDEA funding for those with special needs. Unfortunately, Congress has never provided even half of the funding it has committed to provide.[xv] "Between 2005 and 2017, Congress underfunded public schools in the U.S. by $580 billion –money that was specifically targeted to support 30 million of our most vulnerable students."[xvi]

*The Governor*

The authority of the governor is felt in the areas of policy-making in which the governor can propose legislation, veto legislation, veto appropriations, and set general policies and regulations that apply to all parts of state government. This includes budget recommendations through the appointment authority, which can be felt at all levels of education, including higher education. The governor's influence can also be felt through the staffing of the governor's office for liaison with education and through his or her role in the implementation of federal laws and aid.[xvii] The governor of a state can dictate the budget of schools for the year and he or she can choose the standardized test that every teacher and student will be measured by.

*The Present Result*

It should be clear by now that our education system is a hodgepodge of local, state, and national interests, intentions, and influences. It is an ever-evolving entity that has been marked by tradition, custom, the natural evolution of a country, and uncertainty. From a teacher's standpoint, the biggest problem to conquer for our education system is to get cooks out of the kitchen. There are too many voices, too many demands, too many opinions in the kitchen sink of education. And while some are very well-intentioned and of noble origin, there is a lack of steady direction due to the excess of voices, many of whom shouldn't even be heard.

And make no mistake…presently, politicians have a lot of say in our education system. Politicians at every level of government have a hand in funding our schools, which affects everything from class size, to diversity of the curriculum, to whether your school will have a librarian, or a nurse, or both. State legislators decide how much funding the state will provide and set the formula for distribution – and your governor signs off on that decision. Local school boards decide which academic programs and extra-curricular activities to support across districts. I ask myself, are these people qualified to be making these decisions?[xviii]

## *READ MY LIPS:*

## THERE IS NO ROOM FOR POLITICS IN EDUCATION

The title of this chapter is practically heresy. Some people will read this title and want to come at me with pitchforks. I see burning at the stake, a *witch hunt*, an army marching forward, or worse, a cynical laugh. They will tell me I'm crazy, or that it can't be done, or that I'm just a dreamer. Maybe even a liar –lying to the American public and filling their minds with falsehoods. But please take a moment and consider…

We're living in a country where schools in one district, county, or city look very different from the schools in the neighboring district, county, or city. We're living in a country where how much money is spent on education varies immensely from state to state. We're living in a country where it feels like you can count on the weather with more certainty than the leaders that will take the reins of your state's education system. And the one thing you CAN count on is very little synchronicity and, as a result, very little *accountability*. The wheels of the education machine keep grinding forward, but no one is sure where the machine is headed. And from a teacher's perspective, it's all headed downhill, off the cliff.

President Ronald Reagan and his Secretary of Education, T.H. Bell, released a report back in 1983 warning of "a rising tide of mediocrity" in our education system, realizing that schools weren't able to fill new expectations with their traditional setup. This sparked major political debate in the 1980s and 1990s, thus re-igniting state and federal roles in schools. States reset standards and assessments. The federal government also stepped in aggressively, without constitutional authority, by the way, in an effort to curtail this "rising tide of mediocrity."[xix] Among its recommendations: more rigorous and measurable standards for students and an effective evaluation system for teachers.

But a long time before Reagan, back in 1965, the conversation on education had already begun with President Lyndon B. Johnson. It was through Title I of Johnson's *Elementary and Secondary Education Act* (ESEA) that President Johnson created a clear role for the federal government within education. The Act doubled its expenditure in K-12 education to more than $1 billion in aid. Johnson's intention was a good one: ESEA was supposed to bridge the gap between children in poverty and those from privilege. It called for "equal treatment of children no matter where they reside and attempted to improve reading and math competency for children in poverty."[xx]

President George W. Bush famously reauthorized ESEA and signed the *No Child Left Behind Act* (NCLB) in 2002, which effectively scaled up the federal role in holding schools accountable for student outcomes. It pushed through new policies that focused on standardized testing and teacher accountability, first in state legislatures and then Congress.[xxi]

With NCLB, a bipartisan collaboration, Congress wanted to advance American competitiveness, as there were concerns that the American education system was no longer internationally competitive. Congress also wanted to close the achievement gap between poor and minority students and their more advantaged peers. Under the law, states must test students in Reading and Math in grades three through eight and once in high school. Schools would need to report the results and keep special track of "sub groups" of students, which included English-learners, students in special education, racial minorities, and children from low-income families. "Students in schools that perform below their state's established standards for more than two years must be offered free tutoring, after school programs, or the opportunity to continue their education at a higher-performing government school."[xxii] If schools fell below standards for more than two years in a row, then they left themselves open to the possibilities of state intervention.

And now, fast-forward to December of 2015 when Congress passed, and President Barack Obama signed, the *Every Student Succeeds Act* (ESSA), to replace NCLB. ESSA actually *scaled back* the federal role in K-12 education on everything from testing and teacher quality to low-performing schools. And it gave new leeway to states in calling the shots.[xxiii]

Most recently, on April 26, 2017, President Donald Trump signed the "Education Federalism Executive Order," which requires the United States Department of Education to spend 300 days evaluating the role of the federal government in education. The order is supposed to "determine where the federal government has unlawfully overstepped state and local control." This order comes after a proposal of a 13.5 % cut to the national education budget."[xxiv]

And where does this see-saw of governmental involvement leave us, you ask? Is there any evidence that these standards did anything to slow down the "rising tide of mediocrity?" No. In your opinion, do you feel that public education has seen gains in the last few decades? Your likely answer is "no." This expansion and then contraction from the federal government hasn't served education. Although it seems well-intentioned, federal involvement has continued to muddy the water of education. There are too many cooks in the kitchen. There are too many voices asking for things, which has, in effect, taken time and attention away from the children and driven teachers to checklists and requirements needing to be satisfied.

And what about state politics? Is it any different? No. What about the governor and his or her effect on education? What if a governor is only there for one term? What if a governor is very interested in education or not that interested in education? What kind of an impact do those great four years or not-so-great four years have on the system?

And how much does a governor know about education anyway? How much time does a governor need to spend inside of a classroom or school to make these decisions? No time. The governor doesn't need to know much about schools before deciding how much to spend on them. The governor doesn't need to know much about test-taking before choosing one of the most pivotal assessments for a school system. And to top it all off, a governor typically serves four years, which means that as soon as any governor can begin to get more comfortable with education, if he or she cares enough to, then it's time for a new governor or party at the end of that term to take over.

And this is the grand problem with politics in education. We can't create a consistent, efficient system with any sort of politics involved. Politics brings interested and disinterested parties into the mix, which is also transient. **Education won't elevate above mediocrity in this country until we can dismiss politics from the stage**. It isn't necessary. Politicians haven't spent a majority of their career inside of a classroom or a school system. Therefore, they shouldn't be calling the shots in the system. Education needs to be firmly planted in the hands of those that know education. It should be in the hands of educators that have toiled in the system and really know the ins and outs of the classroom.

# PART II
# LET ME TELL YOU ABOUT TEACHERS

# A Teacher Is Never Bored

Just ask one and they'll tell you. It's almost impossible to be bored. And if you happen to find one that admits to being bored, then she or he could probably also admit that they aren't really invested in their work. I've asked several teachers why they like teaching and many will say that it's the only job they've had where they're NEVER bored. Not even for a minute. It's practically impossible. As soon as you walk into the school hallways, you are recognized. Even if you ignore the children running down the hallway, or if you choose not to remind that student of morning tutoring, the moment you step foot on campus, it's game time. You get into the classroom, turn on the computer, yell "hello" to anyone near you, and run to the bathroom for that last bathroom break until who knows when...you're greeted with multiple students, their parents, absence notes, an argument that broke out just moments before you opened your doors. Can you solve it right now? Someone didn't have time to do their homework...and all before the day's first bell. Eight hours to go.

As the hours tick by, there are countless interruptions: Morning Announcements, Canned Goods Drive, Book Fair schedule is up, teach new Reading skill, teach in small group, rotate centers. May I go to the bathroom? (We've only been in school 15 minutes, but this child claims that he doesn't have time to go to the bathroom when he wakes up in the morning). Oh! And...you'll have to get the door every time someone knocks on your door, for security purposes. Yes, teachers in this day and age have to worry about security. How many times a day do I get my door, did you ask? I can't keep track of course. Who has time for that? But a ballpark average of 20-25 times per day.

You LIVE in minutes as a teacher. You know exactly how many minutes it will take you to sit everyone down, stand everyone back up, line them up in order, and get them quietly and safely to the auditorium, the lunchroom, the music room, or outdoor physical education. And then will begin your rat race to the bathroom, just before you run to get your data binder and head to your next meeting with adults. Don't forget your ream of paper and copies that need to be made. You wouldn't want to waste those precious few minutes going back upstairs to get it when the copy machine is only some feet away from your meeting. INHALE and EXHALE. Make sure to bring your water bottle to this meeting. "You need to stay hydrated," the doctor said. "Teachers are notorious for dehydrating," is what my primary care physician told me. All that talking, not enough drinking, and very limited bathroom breaks. A common response is, "what teacher can afford to go to the bathroom once per hour?" Who will watch your children when nature calls? No one. They've got their own audience to perform for.

I can ring my chime, speak to my classroom neighbor, answer the phone, give commands to two different children, and give a command to the rest of the class –all simultaneously. How many tasks can you perform at once? BORED, you asked???

## What Is a Teacher Worth To You?

What do you pay a person who takes care of your child for seven hours a day and teaches them the fundamentals for the future? How much is it worth to you? And I want to remind you that we are talking about the most precious asset in your life. Wouldn't you agree? Presently, teachers in the U.S. make, on average, between $25-$35 per hour, for approximately 20 children. This means that a teacher is getting paid roughly $1 per hour per child. This means that you, the parents and taxpayers, are paying roughly $7 per day per child in the public school system. What a steal!

For $7 per day, one child will:

>learn the alphabet
>learn to read
>learn how to hold a pencil
>learn how to write
>learn arithmetic
>learn scientific principles
>learn about our country's history
>learn to express themselves through art
>learn how to play an instrument
>exercise
>learn how to play a sport
>learn how to write a sentence
>learn grammar rules
>begin to learn a second language
>learn conflict resolution
>learn teamwork
>learn how to hold utensils
>learn how to proceed in line
>learn how to walk in a line
>learn how to go up and down stairs properly

learn how to type
learn how to write a paragraph
learn what a topic sentence is
learn how to find a main idea
learn how to add up digits
learn how to be a better friend
learn discipline
learn how to take notes
learn how to tie their shoes
learn how to write their name
learn how to sharpen a pencil
learn how to subtract digits
learn what a fraction means
learn about the seasons
learn about respect
learn how to turn on a computer and turn off a computer properly
learn how to use the keyboard
learn how to multiply
hopefully memorize their multiplication facts
learn how to divide
learn how to sing better
learn how to cut and glue properly
learn how to divide with remainders
learn how to use a computer program
learn how to say please and thank you
learn about the phases of the moon
learn about their health
learn what a chorus is in a song
learn about the scientific method
learn about the Thanksgiving story
learn the history behind most national holidays
learn how to add and subtract fractions
learn who Martin Luther King Jr. was
learn how to vote
learn what a food web is
learn about different habitats
think about who they want to be when they grow up on Career Day
learn about who the Presidents were
learn about photosynthesis

learn what an idiom is
learn that a poem can have rhyme or it can be free verse
learn why a shadow occurs
learn the difference between reflection and refraction
learn how to conduct a scientific experiment
learn how to play with a toy or without a toy
learn how to jump rope with a group
learn how to apologize
learn what it means to share
learn how to multiply fractions
learn what the lesson of a story is
learn how to divide fractions
learn how to measure with a ruler
learn the difference between a liter and a gallon
learn how to solve a word problem
learn how to keep their area clean
learn how to organize their desk better
learn the difference between "may I" and "can I"
learn how to mold something with clay
learn how to present a project
learn how to speak in front of others
learn how to plant a seed
learn how to travel in a bus
learn how to tell time
learn what to do if there's ever a fire
learn how to talk about their feelings
learn how to label something
learn how to compare fractions
learn how to solve a two-step word problem
learn how to edit their own writing
learn what a subject is
learn the difference between an uppercase and lowercase letter
learn how to take a test
learn how to bubble an answer sheet
learn what a highlighter is and how to highlight
learn the rules for basketball
learn how to solve three-step word problems
learn what a pentagon is
learn how to play tag

learn the rules to play basketball
learn how to do jumping jacks
learn how to count to 100
learn how to stay seated
learn what an auditorium is
learn how to watch a presentation
learn how to listen
learn how to read aloud
learn how to pack a bag
learn about friction
learn the capitals of most states
learn about the continents and oceans
learn how to cooperate with others
learn how to finish an assignment
learn how to continue an assignment
learn how our government works
learn what a grade is and what it means
learn how to spell a word
learn to find out how much time has elapsed
learn the difference between a cause and an effect
learn how to count money
learn the difference between right and wrong
learn the words to the Pledge of Allegiance.

And the list can go on and on…rarely do adults take the time to think about all that we learn in school. This list focuses on our primary years in school, but will look different if you're a middle school teacher or a high school teacher. All lists will be equally comprehensive and expansive. Let's take a moment to thank all those teachers and school communities that contributed to our unbounded growth and development. We wouldn't be who we are today without it.

So, we have seen some of the value teachers bring to schools, students and society at large. But do teachers receive a fair exchange for the value they bring?

# FINANCIAL PERSPECTIVE

The following are the average annual salaries of certain professionals. For the most part, I chose professions that require extra training or licensure after a college degree, since many teachers boast Master degrees. I also wanted to show the average salary of a realtor and an A/C mechanic in order to demonstrate that you don't need a college degree, in order to make at least as much as a teacher. My purpose here is to show that as things are right now, it just doesn't pay to be a teacher.

Pilot for a large jet..................................................$121,408[xxv]

Heating or Air Conditioning Mechanic...................$44,600[xxvi]

Registered Nurse...................................................$68,450[xxvii]

Physical Therapist................................................$86,520[xxviii]

Veterinarian.........................................................$88,770[xxix]

Pharmacist....................................................$112-119,000[xxx]

Realtor..................................................................$44,090[xxxi]

Accounta..............................................................$76,730[xxxii]

Broker..................................................................$77,000[xxxiii]

Professor............................................................$114,134[xxxiv]

# What To Do About TEACHER BURNOUT

Teachers give of themselves wholeheartedly. They don't really have a choice. From the moment the first bell rings to the moment the last bell rings, teachers are always "on." Imagine walking into a room with twenty or so faces staring at you. Suddenly the spotlight flicks on and you find yourself on stage. "The stage is yours," as they say. Your curtain must rise immediately and your award-winning acting will either make you or break you.

Make no mistake: drama and antics are very effective –and sometimes necessary –with young children. Regardless of the children's age group, teachers have a tremendous amount of effect and impact on a group of children each and every year. And this is no laughing matter. These children will repeat what you say, they will absorb your intention and energy, they will see a teacher for who she or he truly is, and hopefully most will rise to meet the expectation that the teacher places in front of them. And this part is very real. These children aren't characters on a stage acting out a fictitious storyline. Teaching is real life. And there are no "do-overs," for the child nor the teacher.

I worked in a small, elementary public school located in Miami Beach, Florida. You may have heard of the neighborhood. It's called SoBe. But what you may not know is that it's a hodgepodge of very wealthy people interspersed with very poor immigrants. Many of the wealthy residents are foreigners and many of the poor immigrants come from humble backgrounds in Central America. Despite the class disparity in this hodgepodge community, the public school I worked at can almost be considered a small, private school. Alongside several young, active, and well-to-do parents, there is an impressive collection of teachers at this school. We have hard working, intelligent, and highly educated teachers from many different walks of life. Several teachers boast advanced degrees. I've never been to another school with so many gifted minds. Whenever a group of our teachers attends a professional development course, our small staff of less than fifty are the "star students." It never fails to impress me when our staff of teachers is praised by other teachers and other administrators outside of our school community.

I find it heartbreaking that so many of these gifted teachers have reached a point where they no longer want to teach. The breaks aren't long enough. The days aren't short enough. "But you get two months off in the summer!" you might exclaim. Yes, teachers say. What you might not understand is that teachers cram 12 months of work into 10 months. Yes, we do. Our days and weekends are packed with activity for 10 months and then we need two months just to recover. And, by the way, teachers are only paid for 10 months of work. You can choose to break up your gross salary into 12 months, but you're just cutting up your monthly slice of pie a little smaller.

You might ask if it has to do with the children. The answer is "no." Even if you have a good class of motivated students, with few conflictive personalities (which is already reaching for the stars), I have found that the teacher will still burnout. The demands placed upon the teacher, the never-ending list of things to-do becomes too cumbersome for teachers. And I'd like to remind you that most teachers are highly type-A personalities that just LOVE to cross things off their list. In an eight or nine-hour day, a teacher gets approximately 30 minutes of a true break, and 20 minutes of this break is set aside to eat quickly and go to the bathroom. If there happens to be an hour of planning time on that day (because it hasn't been interrupted with other school activities), teachers have to run around doing paperwork, making copies, attending meetings, meeting with parents, meeting with administration, preparing for the next lesson, organizing, or cleaning up. There is never enough time. As a result, every year, we continue to lose more and more of these highly motivated and highly motivational teachers.

How hard are they to replace? Pretty hard. Imagine your A-list, gold star employee ups and quits on you. Then you invest more money and train another. A year later, she also ups and runs. How long would it take (how much would you risk losing) until you questioned whether it was *you* and not *them*? How much training and investment goes into an individual like that? Ask yourself how hard it may be to replace an individual like that?

Now apply this same formula to a teacher. What is at stake? To the future generations, the following is at stake: how much knowledge will be learned, how much growth will be shown that given year, how the school year will be etched into memory? Now let's return to the classroom. Do you remember the names of those teachers that really made an impact in your life? What did she or he teach you? What did you learn from her or him? Now imagine that this individual decided to quit teaching. No more kids would get to experience Mrs. or Mr. Blank. The stakes are high when we speak of our children…of our future.

If it hadn't been for my Kindergarten teacher, Mrs. O'Brien and her generous heart, I would not have learned to read as well as I did. Thanks to her free tutoring, I got to learn English after school as I was an ESOL student, and didn't know a word of English when I started school. And then I got to become a good reader in Kindergarten. And thanks to my good reading abilities, I comprehended things easily and was always a good student. By the Second grade, I sat with the gifted readers. And thanks to always being a good student, I went to one of the most exclusive schools in America. And thanks to my proficiency in Reading and Writing, I get to write this book. How hard is it to replace a teacher of this caliber, you ask? Almost impossible.

# Battered Wife Syndrome

I read a random article on social media, a few years back, about teachers and why they're "walking out." It was from a male's perspective (one of the few) and his thoughts on part of the problem with the system. His viewpoint leaned heavily on the fact that the teaching profession is dominated by women. I checked the numbers. As a matter of fact, about 77% of public school teachers today are female and 80% of these female teachers are white.[xxxv]

And in this system, he argued, these women are treated as if they were in an abusive relationship. And the abusive husband or relationship is the public school system. And at some point there was a hashtag...#battered wife syndrome. Read that again.

I laughed aloud at certain points of this article, in part, because I thought it was a little ridiculous. It depicted teachers as always willing to figure it out, always willing to give more, always willing to resolve, with nothing in their hands. I started analyzing myself as a teacher, and concluded that I don't always fit that criteria, thank God. And then that same week, I saw it with my own eyes, in front of me. I had a fellow teacher and colleague say to me that it was ok that she wasn't going to get some basic needs for the classroom this school year. She had made it through far worse after all. She reminisced about the time, at her last school, when they didn't even have air conditioning for weeks. And, yes, the school was in Miami! I told her that I didn't understand. Even with my limited knowledge of real estate, I was pretty sure that it was illegal to rent out any place that didn't provide air conditioning in Miami-Dade County. How could this basic need not be enforced in schools? We live in a subtropical environment, after all. My concern didn't seem to phase her. It was a passing thought.

And it got me thinking...was this article so ridiculous? Was this idea as out-of-touch as I had initially thought? As teachers, we're asked to do more every year, support more, give more, sacrifice more. At a school meeting, I took a look around the room and all I saw was educators (mostly women) nodding their heads in disapproval and sighing. The look of defeat in their faces. Accepting. Accepting more bad news; more shortages, more cutbacks. As teachers, most of us, immediately jump to thinking about how we're going to make it happen before we even ask ourselves if it's something that we should even make happen, or something that should be happening. It's no wonder that teachers are discouraged, disparaged, and disappointed. It's no wonder that many teachers are fed up.

And then to add fuel to this fire, I found out that other powerful women are saying the same thing. State Representative Attica Scott is currently the only black woman serving in the Kentucky general assembly. She was working hard to encourage more women to run for office in 2018. In her opinion, one of the reasons that teachers, a field that is 77% female, are underpaid, is because they are women. When discussing the #RedforEd movement, she voiced, "this teacher movement is being led mostly by women because most of the teachers are women and it's also one of the reasons why teachers are so under attack…As so often in fields led by women those are the fields that are seen as most vulnerable by politicians…The fact that we see an underrepresentation of women in elected office has a significant part to play in these attacks." In the #MeToo era, Scott thinks that the dynamics of more women running for office could be a powerful force for desperately needed changes in state legislatures.[xxxvi]

Let's ask ourselves, if this were a male-dominated profession as opposed to a female-dominated one, would this be happening? Would men tolerate low wages and high expectations from other men in Tallahassee? Would they stand for it? While I'm not a gambler, I would put a lot of money down at the casino table that, NO, they wouldn't stand for it.

*Maybe it's high time for the women in this profession to take a hard look at what we're saying "yes" to and what we're accepting, and whether or not it should be acceptable. And I say "we" because it's my profession too. I was in this profession that doesn't value or respect teachers for eight years, before I chose to leave it. When are women going to demand that they be valued in this profession? When are women going to demand a professional's pay, respect, and the red carpet rolled out for teachers because teachers are molding the future of this country? Teachers, there is no knight in shining armor that is coming to save us. We don't need saving; we save ourselves. We save ourselves the moment that we believe that we deserve better. And in that moment, the world will rise to meet us. Let's allow for this.*

And, *last but not least*, I would like to acknowledge the men in our profession who give of themselves daily for these children. My experience of male educators is that they are true givers, thinkers, and role models to children. They nurture them just as much as any female does, and many of them serve as father figures to the many children who don't have one at home. They provide a safe space for children, and they often add humor and perspective to an often "heavy" profession. I see you and I appreciate you, male educators. This book is just as much for you.

# PART III
# BEAR WITH ME:
# IT'S GOING TO GET A TAD HEAVY

# Florida:
# One of the WORST States for Education

Florida is such an interesting state. We steal headlines during election season as a leading, hold-your-breath swing state. We've leaned Republican in Presidential elections since the 1950's, been led by a Republican governor for the last eight years, and yet, every so often, pull a Democratic rabbit out of the hat. Democrats predominantly inhabit South Florida, the half that is full of transplants and snow birds from the Northeast. South Florida is made up of Miami-Dade, Broward, and Palm Beach counties. The upper half of the state, especially from Orlando all the way north to Jacksonville and west to the Panhandle, is mostly Republican. From one end to the other, the state looks, feels, and sounds very different.

And when it comes to education, just like in a big election year, this state doesn't disappoint. Florida houses Miami-Dade County, the fourth largest public school district in the nation. This is where I work. We service 356,086 students and employ 18,275 teachers.[xxxvii] Miami-Dade County Public Schools, alone, has a budget of $5.2 billion. Florida also houses Broward County Public Schools, Hillsborough County Public Schools, Orange County Public Schools, and Palm Beach County Public Schools rounding out the largest 10 counties in the country. Wow. Yes, Florida has quite the spotlight. According to Ballotpedia, Florida serviced 2,756,944 students in 2013, a figure that has likely soared in the last six years. In 2013, Florida had the fourth highest total number of schools in the country and the third highest number of charter schools.[xxxviii]

According to the present Republican Governor, Ron DeSantis, Florida has a budget of $90 billion.[xxxix] Think about this number for a second...because it's greater than the budget of many countries in the world. Now, when we turn an eye towards education, U.S. News & World Report ranks Florida as #46 out of 50 in Pre-K-12 education –as in we are only six spots away from being the worst state in the country for Pre-K-12 education. Nope, we aren't the

Northeast region and we are a far cry from the state of Massachusetts, which is consistently rated as the best state for public education. In terms of teacher pay, we were 47th out of 50 in the nation in 2017. By 2018, we were projected to fall to 50th place, according to the Miami-Dade County School Board. As in last place. As in, we are the worst paid teachers in the nation. And we wonder why there's a teacher shortage in Florida? These exact figures on the "scale of bad" seem to vary much depending on who you ask, but the point is clear: for all the money that flows through Florida, it doesn't seem that much stops at education.

What are the factors that dictate state spending? Let's begin with revenue. The amount a school district will spend really depends on the amount it makes. Not surprisingly, a school district will always spend all the money its allocated. Schools that rely mostly on state funding and not local property taxes, generally speaking, have less money to spend. The largest spending capacity will be found with high property values, as they will raise more local property taxes.[xl]

And so how much does Florida actually spend on education, you ask? Well, let's take a look. First and foremost, it's important to note that public school spending varies dramatically from one part of the country to another.[xli] New York is the biggest spender, spending approximately $20,000 per student each year. This price tag includes teacher salaries, support services, and all the other costs associated with public schools. On the other end of the spectrum is Idaho and Utah, which spend a third as much as New York does.

*How a State's Money is Spent on Education*

> *Teacher Salaries*

In this arena, there's even more variance from state to state. New York is the biggest spender coming in at $8,712 per student. To give you an idea of the range of variance, states with fewer teachers and lower wages sometimes spend as little as $3,000 per student. When it comes to teacher salaries, stronger unions play a role, as they generally help teachers secure higher wages. Also, some districts spend more by employing teachers with advanced degrees or more experience, which, of course, means more spending.[xlii]

### ➤ Employee Benefits

Next up are employee benefits. This category includes: teacher pensions, health insurance, tuition reimbursement, and any other employee benefits. Employee benefits for teachers account for $1,700 in spending per pupil nationally and can be as high as $4,660 per student in…you guessed it…New York. Then comes the cost of living. As you would expect, the biggest spenders are in states with a higher cost of living. Costs seem to be highest in District of Columbia, Hawaii and New York according to the Bureau of Economic Analysis.[xliii]

### ➤ Demographics

Continuing on with the analysis is demographics. What does demographics mean exactly? Well, actual students. Some states have more young residents. Take Utah for example. One in every five residents is a public school student in Utah. With so many students, Utah has to be careful to ensure that average costs don't rise to the levels in other states. And then class sizes. Class sizes are directly correlated to demographics. Utah has an average of 28 students per non-departmentalized class while other states like Maine, Tennessee, and Vermont have an average of fewer than 18 students per class.[xliv] Of course, this will also greatly affect a state's wallet.

### ➤ Executive Administration

Second to last, spending on school and executive administration accounts for a small portion of state spending. This figure is about 7% nationally. Not surprisingly, it varies greatly from state to state. Some places like the District of Columbia spend an average of about $1,000 per student whereas the state of Arizona spends an average of $450 per student. More interestingly, however, Massachusetts and New York spend the least on administration. Go figure.[xlv]

> *Miscellaneous*

Lastly, there's a hodgepodge of state and local policies that fall into a black hole of expenses if you will. It's completely unpredictable and dependent per state. States employ varying funding formulas and maintain mandates around special education or other requirements that end up affecting how much districts spend.[xlvi]

And after all of this information, where does Florida stand???? Well, according to the U.S. Census Bureau 2014 Annual Survey of School System Finances, Florida spends $3,214 on instructional salaries per student, $954 on instructional benefits per student, $383 on pupil support per student, $544 on instructional support per student, $78 on general administrative expenses per student, $481 on school administration per student, and $3,102 on "other" expenses per student. For a grand total of $8,756 per student. How much does New York spend, did you ask? Oh yeah…more than $20,000 per student. And the national average was $11,009 per student back in 2014. So…yes, Florida is well under the national average of state spending…with a $90 billion budget. Go figure.

# **CHARTER SCHOOLS: THE BIG DEBATE IN FLORIDA**

*Let's start at the beginning. What is a charter school???*

You would be surprised at how many people who live in this country, including teachers, can't actually define a charter school. And we can't blame anyone for not knowing! The definition of a charter school is confusing, ambiguous, and takes a few minutes to explain yet alone understand.

*Charter schools in Florida are public schools operated independently of public school systems, either by nonprofit or for-profit organizations. Although they are largely publicly funded, charter schools are exempt from many of the requirements imposed by state and local boards of education regarding hiring and curriculum.*[xlvii]

Each charter school also has an actual charter. These "charters" are performance contracts detailing the schools' mission, program, goals, students served, methods of assessment, and ways to measure success. The length of time for which charters are granted can vary from three to fifteen years. At the end of the term, the entity granting the charter may renew the school's contract.

Charter schools are accountable to their sponsor, usually a state or local school board, to produce positive academic results and adhere to the charter contract. The basic concept of charter schools is that they exercise increased autonomy in return for this accountability. They are accountable for both academic results and fiscal practices to several groups: the sponsor that grants them, the parents who choose them, and the public that funds them.[xlviii] I will also add, however, that there seems to be an awful lot of disagreement about how much accountability a charter school *actually* undertakes.

## *The confusion around charter schools*

When a teacher works for a charter school, their pay check is NOT coming from the school district; it's coming from an administrative entity that the charter school must hire to run it, or the charter school, itself, if it has been set up as a non-profit. According to the National Alliance for Public Charter Schools, a charter school advocacy group, the majority of charter schools (two-thirds of the approximate 7,000 charter schools in the nation) operate independently from any management organization as non-profit entities. The remaining third of schools utilize some sort of management organization for the sake of efficiency and growth. Management is necessary in order to streamline operations and increase funding. And there are two types of management: Charter Management Organizations (CMOs) and Education Management Organizations (EMOs).

Now, here, I have found conflicting information. According to the National Alliance for Public Charter Schools, CMOs, which include well-known charter school networks such as KIPP, IDEA, and Harmony Public Schools, are organizations with a non-profit status. EMOs, with networks like Academica and National Heritage Academies, are management organizations with a for-profit tax status, that charge the schools a management fee for their services. There is, however, contradicting information. According to an article in the Washington Post published in May of 2019, CMOs are for-profit. It goes so far as to say, "the non-profit charter school becomes a 'pass-thru' for the for-profit corporation to staff the school, provide fiscal, procurement and legal operations, and even be the landlord."[xlix]

To use as a frame of reference, in 2013, there were roughly 3,609 "regular" schools in Florida and 581 charter schools.[l] This number has risen to just over 655 total charter schools in Florida (the third most in the country) as of the 2017-18 school year, according to the Florida Department of Education.[li] These schools enrolled approximately 282,500 students, and presently, Miami-Dade County oversees 134 charter schools.

## *What's so special about Florida?*

Florida has become one of the guinea pigs for Betsy DeVos and President Trump's charter school solution. The solution agrees with the ideology of closing down public schools and giving charter, private, or religious schools public funding. For those of you who don't know, Education Secretary Betsy DeVos is a long-time proponent of vouchers and other vehicles that drain critical funding for public schools and send it to an array of unaccountable private entities."[lii] DeVos "is a vocal advocate of cutting education spending and freeing up federal dollars to expand charter and voucher programs nationwide. And, for your information, charter schools have expanded dramatically since their introduction in 1992, and currently serve about five percent of the nation's students."[liii]

> ### *The Schools of Hope*

In June of 2017, former Governor Rick Scott signed HB7069 into law, which was a massive education bill giving charter schools county tax money for their facilities and a larger share of federal dollars for low-income students.[liv] These charter schools would receive public funding, but must not be located anywhere near the school that closed down or service the children that were being serviced by the low-performing public school. Huh?

"The $140 million Schools of Hope program gives charter school operators money to locate in areas where elementary and middle schools have been rated D or F for at least three years straight. Right now there are 18 in Broward County, 10 in Miami-Dade County and none in Palm Beach County."[lv] "Charter schools will have to meet certain state criteria to participate, including academic success in other locations and a history of serving low-income students. The program also includes money for 25 low-performing traditional schools in the state to do turnaround programs before charter schools would be allowed to come in. The program, as well as other provisions in the law, are expected to lead districts to close some perennially failing schools."[lvi] So far, so good. Who doesn't agree with replacing low-performing schools with better ones?

This new bill signed into law "gives high-performing charter schools more flexibility to expand. Right now, a high-performing charter school is allowed to easily duplicate its program in another area in the state, but it's limited to one additional school a year. The new law allows charter school operators to open multiple schools per year if they go into areas where traditional students are performing poorly. The law also requires districts to use a standard state contract for charter schools, which limits the number of restrictions a school district can place on a charter school."[lvii] Now this part of the law raises some flags for me because I could see how charter schools can start popping up everywhere without any evidence to support their development.

Why did legislators think these pro-charter school measures were needed? Two main issues are cited: fairness and poor results at some traditional schools. "[Legislators] in Florida argue that charter schools should be entitled to the same dollars as traditional schools, since they are also public schools. They allege that districts focus too much on bureaucracy rather than students, particularly those in D- and F-rated schools.[lviii] I would like to chime in here and add that legislators in Tallahassee are labeling charter schools the same as traditional schools. I question this logic, as most charter schools in Florida are being run by a private entity, and not being held to the same standards as a traditional public school. I do, however, agree with the fact that there is way too much bureaucracy within the entire school system.

So how will these "Schools of Hope" in Florida be better than the low-performing public school, you ask? No clue. The bills signed into law by former Governor Rick Scott don't mention how these charter schools will be a better option for our children or our state. Moreover, if you do a little research, the results of charter schools are questionable at best. After the 2016-2017 school grades were released, less than 1% of traditional public schools earned F's, but 3.4% of charter schools did earn F's. This means that charter schools were more than three times as likely to fail.[lix] In addition, over 300 charter schools in Florida closed down due to poor management, which happens frequently with charter schools.

## *Follow the money*

And now...the money. This new law in Florida also requires district schools to split with charters, equally, the local money each district raises to pay for capital expenditures. Capital expenditures means the money that pays for physical repairs and school improvements. "The state has allocated money in recent years for charter schools to build or lease facilities, provide maintenance and buy computers and school buses. This year, 556 charter schools shared $75 million, which charter schools have said covers only a fraction of what they need, which is not surprising. State law allows, but does not require, school districts to share local school property tax dollars. While a few school districts have shared this revenue, South Florida districts have not. The state law will allow charter schools access to county dollars in addition to any state allocations."[lx] And, finally, local charter schools will receive a percentage of property taxes, based on student enrollment. Here is one reason that charter schools are so concerned with student enrollment.

Not surprisingly, charter schools say this money will be welcome. The charter school system run by the city of Pembroke Pines now collects two-thirds of what traditional schools receive, said city vice mayor Angelo Castillo when interviewed. "Every year we have to pull a rabbit out of a hat to keep the school from going bankrupt," he said.[lxi] It takes a lot of money to run a school so I don't believe that statement is an exaggeration.

But what happens if the charter school doesn't make it, financially, with this new law? What happens to this money allocated for these charter schools? "The law says charter schools must be in operation for at least two years before they can collect capital dollars. Any buildings owned by a charter school board would revert back to the school district. However, many charter schools rent their space from for-profit management companies, and those buildings would stay with the owner. In laymen's terms: the money is lost. As most charter schools lease their spaces, the provision about "any buildings owned revert back to the school district" of this new law doesn't really apply.

There was significant uproar before the bill was signed into law a couple of years ago. Teachers came out in protest of this bill that slid secretly by the legislature. Even the Superintendents Association wrote a comprehensive, honest, and unifying letter to then Governor Scott showing their opposition to this bill...that was nonetheless signed into law.

## *The dark side of charter schools*

As previously mentioned, the Washington Post published an article in May of 2019 which took a hard look at charters and what they have meant in Florida. Carol Burris, originally a New York high school principal who now serves as executive director of the Network for Public Education has been writing about school choice for years on a blog. She just co-authored a report where her organization published that the federal government has wasted up to $1 billion on charter schools. These schools either never opened, or opened and then closed due to mismanagement and other reasons, and, in her opinion, the Education Department doesn't adequately monitor how its grant money is spent.[lxii]

Between 2006 and 2014, there were 502 charter schools in Florida that received grants from the Department of Education. According to the U.S. Department of Education Charter Schools Program (CSP), these Florida charter schools were awarded a total of nearly $92 million in federal funds in the span of these eight years. To one's dismay, at least 184 of those schools are now closed, or never opened at all. These defunct charter schools received $34,781,736 in federal "seed" money that was essentially lost.[lxiii] Furthermore, there are several examples of charter schools that were already insolvent or nearly shut down that were still receiving grant money from the federal government.

According to the article, one of the primary reasons for the explosive growth and failure of charter schools in Florida is that nearly half are run by for-profit Charter Management Organizations (CMOs).[lxiv] In fact, due to these concerns regarding the relationships between charter schools and their CMOs, the Office of the Inspector General (OIG) of the U.S. Department of Education conducted an audit of those relationships in three states between 2011-2013. Florida was one of the states audited.

> ## *The results?*

The Office of the Inspector General (OIG) audited five charter schools in Florida. Three of the five schools belonged to Academica, a for-profit charter management company with schools in five states and the District of Columbia. Academica services 126 charter schools in Florida alone, including Pitbull's famous SLAM charter chain. As a CMO, Academica serves in a similar capacity to a school district's staff and board's role in managing a traditional public school. The OIG audit of three Academica schools, which were Excelsior, Mater High, and Mater East, raised many questions. The auditors found that the Board of Excelsior allowed Academica to make most decisions and that the for-profit CMO participated in all charter board meetings and made recommendations to the board. OIG's audit of the two Mater schools revealed related party transactions between Academica and a real estate company that leased both buildings and security services to the schools. The investigation found inappropriate transactions among the CMO, real estate companies, and the charter schools. In addition, these real estate companies and LLC's that serviced these charter schools were found to be owned by the Zulueta brothers, the founders of both the Mater Academies and Academica.

For your information, by 2010, the Zulueta brothers controlled more than $115 million in Florida tax-exempt real estate with the companies that leased to the charter schools, collecting about $19 million in lease payments. Many of these schools paid rents well above expected rates. Academica not only benefited from renting real estate it owned, it also sold payroll, employer services, construction services, equipment leasing and school services to the schools.

With this complicated web of conflicts of interest, one would think that Academica would have been scaled back. Not at all. Deep-pocket contributions to Florida lawmakers have shielded Academica and other for-profit CMOs from regulations, not to mention direct ties to legislators. Take for example, Erik Fresen, former Florida House Representative, who was Fernando Zulueta's brother-in-law. Fresen, a former lobbyist for Academica, served as chairman of the House Education Appropriations even while working as a consultant for a firm called Civica, which had contracts with Academica schools. During his eight years in the legislature, Fresen never filed his taxes, which resulted in a 60-day prison sentence after he left office.

And Academica continues to expand. Big names like Somerset, Pitbull's SLAM, and Mater charter school chains use Academica as their CMO. Even the Biden family is mentioned. Frank Biden, Joe Biden's brother, was previously associated with another for-profit charter chain known as Maverick. Nearly every Maverick charter in the state has closed. And despite all of the problems with Florida charter schools, in 2016, the U.S. Department of Education gave Florida a three-year grant for almost $71 million. This Washington Post article clearly states its entitled opinion: "we are all subsidizing the charters that feed the for-profit chains."[lxv]

## *Final thoughts*

As legislators battle it out on the battlefield of traditional v. privatization, *less* money is being split between the two camps, thus producing even more dismal results in our system. And once again, I'd like to point out, most of these legislators making key education decisions for the future of our country have never set foot in a classroom, other than to drop their own children off at school.

*In my humble opinion: At the end of the day, if you choose to overlook some of the dealings mentioned above, and whether you side with traditional public schools or you're a supporter of charter schools, there is no denying that there is a lot of sharing of funds happening with an ever-decreasing education budget around the country.* Period.

# On Unions

## "One for All and All for One"

The word *union* has crossed my path in short sections of various history books throughout my education. I remember it had a rather easy definition to memorize, but the concept is quite abstract. My first real introduction to a union was while watching a documentary about education entitled, "Waiting for Superman." Based on this documentary, unions are bad. They are this big, invisible behemoth of a thing that protects bad teachers because they can. In the film, I remember that due to unions, bad teachers are really hard to fire. So hard to fire, actually, that there's a room in some building in Washington D.C., where felonious teachers go every day to read the newspaper for eight hours a day because they can't *actually* be fired. Now this got my attention and raised my eyebrows. Who's ever heard of this? What are these so-called unions...?

But as time passed and I became more acquainted with unions, by actually working for the school system, I began to understand more of their purpose. Unions are in place in order to *fight*. You see, the school system, like other public service professions, seems to be at battle constantly. **The people, or politicians, who pay teachers, police officers, firefighters, or other civil servants seem to always want to short-change them.** There's a *don't let them take more from us* mentality. The unions are there, in theory, to ensure that these civil servants don't continue to get robbed. Observing the teaching profession from an outsider's point of view, which at the beginning of my career was relatively neutral, I saw a combative relationship between the teachers vs. the system. The system seems to be the unfair opponent: wily, clever, and carries a big stick. The teachers, on the other hand, seem like bleeding heart liberals that are beat without even the need for a big stick due to their compassionate, big hearts. Teachers seem a lot like *victims*. They get things taken away from them, they often get short-changed, and they get taken advantage of a lot. And to top it all off, there's a model of scarcity that many have gotten used to. What I mean by that is a "that's *my* pencil" kind of attitude. An attitude that there won't be enough pencils and, therefore, you need to hoard as many pencils as possible to make it through the school year. And while this may seem ridiculous to some, most teachers are probably nodding their heads right now in agreement.

As a result of all of this analysis, I was very resistant to joining the teacher's union of Miami-Dade County, also known as the United Teachers of Dade (UTD). I admit that my only real knowledge was coming from a biased documentary, but I couldn't understand needing to pay dues (approx. $1,000 annually) when our teacher salaries were already so low. And then a couple of years passed and I saw veteran teachers frustrated and angry. Rick Scott was governor at the time and the "steps" system, which had dictated a teacher's road to retirement for the past decade or two, was all of a sudden dissolved. Teachers felt robbed. They had been waiting to reach those final "steps," according to the system. They should have finally been earning a decent salary in the $70,000 range before retiring. And now, suddenly, it had been taken away. They blamed the union because they *let* it happen and some of these teachers had been dues-paying members for decades. Not only was I avoiding the union representatives that showed up at school once a year or so, but I found myself to be defensive around them.

> ### *Unions and Florida*

Let me explain something special about Florida. Florida is a "right-to-work" state. This means that employers have a lot of power to hire and fire as they see fit.[lxvi] In a teacher's case, this means that an employer really doesn't need to take into account if the teacher is a union member or not because union membership is not compulsory. It won't even cross a principal's mind when hiring. If, however, this were a state like New York, then it would be very different. You see in a state like NY, whether the teacher is a union member or not matters a lot. In NY, there is compulsory union membership, which many states, like Florida, don't allow. This means that NY can tell that newly hired teacher that she or he *must* join the union. On the flip side, NY also allows its employees to organize, bargain, and *strike*.[lxvii] In sum, teachers in NY have compulsory union membership which allows for them to rise up and strike at any moment without fearing that they will lose their jobs. *In Florida, it's the opposite. There isn't compulsory union membership, but if teachers strike, then they are at-risk of losing their jobs.*

Years passed and I befriended a firefighter who started talking to me about union membership and why it's important. He started detailing how police officers and firefighters unite on these matters, especially in his home state of NY. As a result, police officers and firefighters in NY are well paid. Teachers do better too, for several other reasons as I've detailed in previous chapters, but the power of the unions plays a large role. I started doing some research and talking to some local firefighters and I realized that, generally speaking, police officers and firefighters are better compensated due, mostly, to the simple fact that their union membership is that much greater. These civil servants understand that united they stand and divided they fall. Ironically, educators are stuck analyzing their union membership endlessly, which contributes to their poor compensation. And in most cases, the difference in compensation is big.

After much discussing and mulling over with a new perspective, I decided to join the union at the very end of the 2017-2018 school year. I joined, primarily, because Miami-Dade County was on the brink of losing its teacher union. A bill was passed, early in 2018, which stated that if the union didn't reach "50% plus one" membership by the summer, the union would be dissolved until the next year. I looked into what this meant *exactly*. My research led me to find out that, as a result, no one would bargain for the teachers' contract, which meant that the city or county would give teachers the bare minimum. And if UTD was dissolved, there would still be organizations competing for the *job* of bargaining for the teachers' contract. They would compete with one another for every teacher's money and attention. And once one of them was decided the *winner* with the most membership, then that organization or unit would simply replace UTD and the cycle would start over. According to the cycle and system, therefore, there would always be a union of sorts. There was no escaping it.

As part of my research, I looked into districts or counties where the unions had been dissolved as the Florida legislature was trying to do.

> ### *What happens if we lose union representation?*

Research shows that localities without union representation for teachers do very poorly on contracts, which is probably obvious to many. They are among the worst paid. For example, Wisconsin. Wisconsin gutted its union through Act 10 which was passed by the state legislature in 2011. Just like Florida, Wisconsin is a right-to-work state which means that being a member of a union and paying dues is voluntary. So what happened in Wisconsin? "Teachers have seen lower pay, reduced pension, health insurance benefits, and higher turnover as educators hop from one district to another in search of raises."[lxviii] According to the left-leaning Center for American Progress Action Fund, the numbers are clear. "In the five years since Act 10 was passed, median salaries for teachers in the state have fallen by 2.6% and median benefits declined 18.6%. In addition 10.5% of public school teachers in Wisconsin left the profession after the 2010-2011 school year…the exit rate remains elevated, at 8.8%."[lxix] Nothing positive was left after the dissolution of the union in Wisconsin.

And then there's North Carolina. A colleague and friend of mine recently moved over there in pursuit of a greater quality of life. She loved North Carolina so much that she was willing to live with the sizable pay cut when transferring from Florida to North Carolina, as a veteran public school teacher. She figured that with the cost of living difference, things would balance out. But then she started to experience the day-to-day toil of living without union representation. There were Jewish holidays that weren't observed, a personal day will cost you $50 over there (as in you must PAY money to take a personal day), and long school meetings until 5 pm because administrators can keep you that long over there (keep in mind that teachers start their school day earlier than most professionals). Slowly, but surely, the gap between the states became wider for my friend. Finally, when local voters in Miami-

Dade County passed Referendum 362 adding funds to teacher salaries, the pay cut became too wide. We're talking about $30,000, which is no small sum to anyone, especially a teacher. And so my friend moved back to Miami-Dade County, with a greater appreciation for the union, and a renewed sense of spirit for the few years she has left before she can retire.

## *Food for Thought*

Even with the evidence above, I can't help but ask myself, "why do we need teacher unions?" Why do we need something set up to bargain for us? Why do we need contracts? If we remove politics from education altogether, will we even need unions? No one can answer this question for me. And I guess it's because it's never happened. We're continuing a cycle, a program, a way of doing things, simply because we haven't stopped long enough to notice if it still works.

I realize the historical importance of labor unions and the great protection it afforded workers in this country. There was a need for a collective power to protect the rights of the working class due to the Industrial Revolution. Things have changed, however, since the original model of unions; unions were white and male and industrial.[lxx] Haven't we evolved past this, yet? Don't we want to evolve past this?

If we were to remove politics from the equation, would we need to hire a group of people to negotiate a contract for us? Let's think big. If we had a board composed of past educators in charge of education for the state or district, then would we need someone to negotiate a contract for teachers with this group of former teachers? Could we save money if we didn't need a union? Could a select group of teachers represent the whole group? Could this group be voted in? If we funneled in tax dollars differently, would we still have to bargain with state and local governments? Why should we have to bargain with the city? Doesn't the city, district, and state align with teachers and education and what they need? Why is it set up to clash? It feels as though city or state interests are pitted against an education budget. Has anyone bothered to ask why?

## *What I Dislike About Unions*

My misgivings on unions stem from over-protection. Unfortunately, often, the union becomes an umbrella for misconduct and pettiness. I can understand the purpose of negotiating a contract, but I can't understand protecting a bad teacher at all costs, or arguing about the letter of a contract. The reputation that a union carries for a teacher is that she or he will be protected from any lawsuit and/or problem that may arise. Most teachers know that it will be extremely difficult to get fired if she or he belongs to the union. The other role often assigned to the union representative is that of law-giver. She or he will walk around school with the teachers' contract in-hand fighting petty arguments (fun fact: a teacher's contract is the size of a small book using a very small font full of legal writing). Your union representative will fight the principal should he or she want to take up an extra hour of your time that's not under contractual agreement. Again, there's a focus on scarcity.

This is where my blood boils. It's with facts about arguing over the letter of a contract or protecting teachers that shouldn't be teaching where I can't condone union action. I understand that this may represent a minority of union actions, but I can't stand the idea of doing something irrational simply because it's a rule. If the school or my principal has a need that falls a little outside of my contract, then I believe in a quid pro quo. This is the legal term which means a "give and take." There should always be room for flexibility, in my opinion. The frame of mind for teachers needs to move away from a "us" vs. "them" mentality, towards a teamwork mentality, or an "it takes a village to raise a child" mentality.

And I can never support paying a teacher who doesn't fulfill her or his responsibilities and obligations. A teacher should be treated as any other highly educated professional. There are responsibilities and duties that must be fulfilled satisfactorily in order to keep your job, just like in any other profession or company. This idea of equality will also hold true when speaking about compensation and promotion. The idea of a teacher having lifetime job security is one that I'm very willing to sacrifice for a more respected and valued profession in our present society.

And last but not least, states are all over the place when it comes to unions. This current situation helps to spread great disparity amongst states and therefore teachers. It creates more division amongst teachers. Again the lesson comes up: divided we fall.

## *A Bombshell Ruling*

On June 27, 2018, the U.S. Supreme Court ruled in *Janus v. AFSCME* that public employees now have the right to fully opt out of paying membership dues to labor groups that collectively bargain on their behalf. This means, essentially, that every state has become like a right-to-work state. Union membership can't be compulsory anymore…in any state. What? Now what? Teachers with strong union membership in their states are viewing this as a big blow to the teaching profession. One of the concerns is that it may "pit teachers against one another, as those who opt to save $800 a year in membership fees still benefit from the contracts that their local unions negotiate on their behalf, as well as many of the same benefits afforded to dues-paying members."[lxxi] Carmen Barbone, a high school English teacher in Minnesota, worries about protections she depends on now that unions will be weakened. What's to stop "her principal from replacing her with two less experienced teachers for less pay?"[lxxii] Ironically, this court decision comes as millions of Americans recommit to their unions and launch new organizing drives. Support for labor unions has risen to its highest level in years. This decision will affect millions of workers in nearly half of the states that require payments from nonmembers to cover the cost of collective bargaining.[lxxiii] Agustina Paglayan, a political economist who studies how governments around the world choose education policies, is predicting "a wave of strikes in a lot more states." According to her analysis, teachers are marching in states where unions are weak because "they have much less to lose."[lxxiv] What is the future of unions then? It seems that the Supreme Court is forcing this question, and NOW.

## *So what happened, finally?*

To conclude my story, I became a union member. I joined late in the 2017-2018 school year because the union was being threatened with extinction and I had done enough research to know that this wouldn't be favorable. I joined in late April of 2018 to help support the "50% plus one" membership that the Florida legislature was calling for.

As irony would have it, fast-forward four months later, and I became the school's union steward. There were some major changes with administration that summer, and as a result, our union steward left the school. No one really wanted the position. And a few teachers had noticed that I was keeping up-to-date with news affecting teachers and that I knew something about the subject. And, therefore, I was voted in as union steward for the 2018-2019 school year.

Through the course of the school year, I got to see the union up close and personal. I even applied for and was accepted into the Teacher Leaders Program, where I had more interaction with union leadership and teacher leaders from around the district. My experience of the union is that it means well. It is well-intentioned and intelligent, but also disorganized and incompetent at times. While I like the leadership presently, the union is like a giant, unruly ship that has a good captain, but not enough hands on deck. The few paid positions that I met were willing and competent, but I would hear teachers complain often about their negative experiences with others. It doesn't seem like everyone is on the same page most of the time. Moreover, there are several stewards and leaders that take on leadership positions and don't really have the time to because they're still full-time teachers. Let's be clear: the bulk of active members in the union take on a second unpaid job, essentially, and are therefore limited with time and their results. The union is comparable to a very slow-moving machine that expends a lot of energy, but can't seem to direct that energy in order to actually move forward.

***TIMING is everything.***

***It's a revolution.***

***The litmus test for the nation.***

There is a movement that has begun. If you've paid any attention to the teacher's plight in the last few years, you'll know there has been a string of strikes around the country, and a #RedForEd movement. You might have even seen teachers wearing red shirts on the news, symbolizing their dissatisfaction with the state of schools in their particular state, and going on strike. In 2015, 29 out of 50 states provided less school funding than in 2008. Since state funding fuels nearly half of the nation's K-12 spending, these cuts have had huge implications. School boards have been forced to cut programs, increase class sizes, or raise more money locally. [lxxv]

Educators in states with weak unions (mostly Republican-dominated states) have started organizing in a grassroots fashion. Teachers are now connecting through social media and taking matters into their own hands, as they're realizing that their union representation isn't doing enough for them.

Newsweek published an article in July 2018 describing this cause. The article spotlights on the plight of teachers around the country, following the trajectory through the state of West Virginia. The story follows a teacher named Tina Adams. Tina is a veteran teacher, having taught for 15 years. Still, she was making only $47,000 a year, which happens to be $12,000 less than the national average of teacher salaries. She's also a mother of six. Clearly, her paycheck was not enough to support her family. To add injury to insult, the state's governor, Jim Justice, was backing out on his promise for a teacher salary increase and a halt on raising insurance premiums. And so, Tina Adams started organizing. She took her protest to the state Capitol in Charleston, along with hundreds of educators from four counties who walked out of their classrooms for one day to demand better pay and benefits. This day, marked as "Fed-Up Friday," didn't do much with the Republican-led Legislature, but the protest made a mark on local headlines and sparked a fire in West Virginia. [lxxvi]

Three weeks later, teachers from around the state joined the wave. For nine days, every public school in West Virginia shut down, as thousands of teachers from all 55 counties made their trek to Charleston, making it the longest strike in the state's history. After nine days of the teacher walkout, on March 6, 2018, Governor Justice of West Virginia signed a pay deal earning teachers a 5% raise. The governor also pledged to set up a task force to address state insurance problems, with Ms. Adams by his side at the signing.

And this was only the beginning. Many other educators in many other states were inspired by this movement in West Virginia. The fire caught wind and spread. Other states that rose up in what's been called the "Education Spring" (spring of 2018) include Arizona, Oklahoma, Kentucky, Colorado, Virginia, and North Carolina.

## *Education Spring of 2018*

> ### *Kentucky*

In Kentucky, after lawmakers slipped changes to teachers' pensions into a bill about sewage, thousands of educators protested. The pension changes were signed into law, nonetheless, but educators secured an increase to per pupil funding to $4,000 per student, which is the highest dollar amount ever appropriated. [lxxvii]

> ### *Oklahoma*

Oklahoma educators led a nine-day #RedForEd strike that ended when lawmakers approved a historic tax increase (their first in 28 years) to pay for $6,100 average pay raises for teachers and $1,250 raises for education support professionals. The state legislature's decades-old tax cuts for the wealthy had cost Oklahoma's public schools about $1 billion each year. [lxxviii] At the end of the day, there was a $50 million increase in education funding, which still fell short from the $150 million needed. As a result, a record number of educators ran for state office in 2018. [lxxix]

### ➢ Colorado

Colorado public schools were underfunded by $822 million, and per-student funding was $2,700 below the national average. Similarly, the underfunding stemmed from corporate tax breaks. After Colorado educators rallied, several bills were signed into law that increased education funding and addressed the educator shortage. [lxxx]

### ➢ Arizona

In late April 2018, about 75,000 Arizona Education Association (AEA) members and allies held the largest educator walkout in history, flooding the streets of Phoenix while demanding more state funding. No state in the nation has cut more school funding than Arizona. Lawmakers have slashed school support by 36.6% between 2008-2015, according to the non-partisan Center on Budget and Policy Priorities (CBPP). In 2018, school funding was 13.6% less than in 2008. Arizona lawmakers, like many others, had opted in favor for corporate tax cuts rather than investments in public education.[lxxxi] After a six-day walkout, Arizona educators secured a law that raises teachers' pay by 20% over the next three years and increases funding for support staff, new textbooks, upgraded technology, and infrastructure.[lxxxii]

### ➢ North Carolina

North Carolina was next. Hundreds of schools closed for the *March for Students and Rally for Respect* in Raleigh, N.C. in May 2018. In a preemptive strike, House Speaker Tim Moore had stated that budget leaders in the House and Senate had already approved a 6.2% increase in teacher salaries for the upcoming fiscal year. Moore told reporters that this would be the fifth year that teacher pay has increased in North Carolina. According to the National Education Association, however, these recent salary increases, once adjusted for inflation, actually meant that teachers had lost 9.4% in pay since 2009.<sup>lxxxiii</sup> North Carolina educators secured a 6.2% raise for teachers after 20,000 educators walked out.

> ## Los Angeles, California (2019)

In January 2019, more than 30,000 members of United Teachers Los Angeles (UTLA) joined the movement and took a stand for their 600,000 kids in Los Angeles public schools. Some of the major problems addressed included: class sizes of 45 or more students, 40% of schools with a nurse only one day a week, and inadequate funding for key programs such as early childhood education and special education. After a six-day strike, educators secured a 6% raise, more school nurses and librarians, smaller class sizes, a commitment to reduce testing by half, investment in community schools, and a pathway toward charter school expansion caps.<sup>lxxxiv</sup>

## #RedForEd

Well over 400,000 educators and other public school supporters participated in the #RedForEd walkouts, protests, and rallies championing education.<sup>lxxxv</sup> This movement was hoping to deliver pro-public education voters and candidates to the polls in fall 2018 and, in the long term, protect the nation's public schools and transform unions. Educators, students, parents, and community members are fed up of hearing that one school counselor is enough for 1,430 students, or that the state can only afford to have four days in the school week (yep –hundreds of districts have been forced to cut back), or that teachers are selling their blood to pay their bills.<sup>lxxxvi</sup>

"Education [was] one of the most pressing issues of the 2018 midterm elections, and both parties were rushing to embrace teachers, particularly in states like West Virginia, host to a number of competitive House and Senate races that did help determine control of Congress in November. Across the country, dozens of former and current educators ran for state legislative seats –34 in

Kentucky alone –and gave Democrats hope in some of the most conservative corners in the nation." lxxxvii

Even the National Education Association was drastically expanding the number of community-organizing trainings for teachers around the country. The organization launched a new program to instruct educators how to run for office. "'It really is a which-side-are-you-on moment,' says Randi Weingarten, president of the NEA's counterpart, the American Federation of Teachers. 'You see on the ground, all over America, teachers taking action and having faith these actions will actually change things. At the same time, it's pretty clear the powers that be in this country are against unions and worker power. We are in a race.'"lxxxviii

Despite the majority change in the House, most educators that ran for office in November of 2018 lost their races. According to an Education Week analysis, 177 current teachers ran for state legislative seats across the country. Of those teacher candidates, only 42 won the general elections. lxxxix There were boosts to education funding, especially in Oklahoma where lawmakers increased formula funding per student by 19%, mostly because education was so grossly underfunded there. Arizona, North Carolina, and West Virginia also saw gains, ranging from 3% to 9% per student, which is progress, but very minor progress.xc

### How did we get here?

"Teaching was never a way to get rich, but it was long considered a solid and respectable middle-class occupation. Over the past few decades, though, policymakers, have chipped away at the economic and moral status of educators. As lawmakers embraced more and more privatization –for example, voucher programs that allowed parents to spend public school dollars on private education –the Great Recession ravaged state coffers, depriving schools of even more support. States cut K-12 education deeply to balance their budgets, and districts laid off hundreds of thousands of employees. Most haven't bounced back. According to an analysis by the Center on Budget and Policy Priorities, a left-leaning think tank, 29 states were spending less per student in 2015 than they were in 2008; in more than half of those states, the cut was 10% or more."[xci]

"That has translated into larger class sizes and fewer resources for teachers. At the same time, educators' salaries remained flat or sank, devoured by inflation. In 39 states, the average teacher made less in 2016 than in 2010 after adjusting for inflation, an Axios analysis of federal data found. Meanwhile, the pay gap between educators and their non-teaching, college-educated peers is widening. In 1994, teachers earned about 2% less than comparably qualified workers in the private sector. By 2015, the 'teacher pay penalty' had grown to 17%, according to the left-of-center Economy Policy Institute."[xcii]

"'It used to be a good job, with a reliable pension, health care and good wages,' says Secky Fascione, a former NEA organizing director. 'Not anymore. It used to be a profession, but now it's more of a service job.'" [xciii]

An annual MetLife teachers' poll found educators' job satisfaction dropped from 62 to 39% between 2008 and 2012, the last year teachers were surveyed. Unsurprisingly, many are dropping out of the profession. Between 2009 and 2014, teacher enrollment nationwide dropped from 691,000 to 451,000, a 35% reduction, according to the nonprofit Learning Policy Institute. Nearly 8 percent of educators leave the workforce each year, the majority of them before retirement age. Meanwhile, the student population is booming."[xciv]

Teachers have started moving to surrounding states for higher pay, or left teaching altogether. Will Daniels, a model teacher in West Virginia that worked with at-risk high school students describes how teachers feel. "It was my goal to be the best teacher out there", he says, "but slowly, through the climate in general and the bureaucracy, I had the wind taken out of my sail."
After working as a teacher for seven years, Daniels left at the end of this school year to run a lawn care business. He figures he can be more helpful creating jobs in the community than struggling in a classroom. He's part of a trend: West Virginia had more than 700 teacher vacancies this year, forcing administrators to combine

grades and assign teachers to subjects for which they're not trained.[xcv] The teacher shortage has grown so acute that the nonpartisan Learning Policy Institute (LPI) estimates that hundreds of thousands of U.S. students are being taught this year [2019] by unqualified or under-qualified instructors. "Short-term strategies, like hasty certification programs, likely worsen the problem, and under-prepared teachers leave at two to three times the rate of well-prepared teachers."[xcvi]

And "to cope with the educator shortage [in West Virginia], lawmakers introduced a bill to lower teacher certification standards to fill job openings more easily." By early 2018, educators in West Virginia were clearly fed up. "It wasn't simply the lack of money. It was the lack of respect."[xcvii]

*"While I don't live in West Virginia or have any clue of what it's like to live there, I can understand and relate to what teachers there are going through because it's a symptom nationwide. While our state and local governments give us the impression that things can be very different depending on where you are, the reality for teachers is the same everywhere. Most state governments are doing a very poor job of funding education. It seems as though there isn't enough money to support a decent education for children, and teachers are asked to do more and more every year with less and less. The teaching "profession" is so poorly paid that it's hard to respect teachers as actual professionals.*

*I can't tell you how many teachers have told me that they will go into real estate or tutor privately at a high rate per hour to get out of the classroom. And they are so much happier doing that instead, including myself. There is nothing wrong with becoming a realtor, running a lawn business, or tutoring privately. The shame is that we're losing out on good teachers because teachers can't make ends meet on a teaching salary, and they work particularly hard for that insufficient salary. It just adds insult to injury.*

*This movement will come to a head. The teaching profession is so disgruntled and unhappy that it's only a matter of time. Either the nation takes some more time to reach a critical mass with a major teacher shortage for the country OR teachers rise up and demand more sooner. And then it's up to the country whether or not it will listen."*

Michael Hansen, a political economist at the Brookings Institution, has predicted future states at risk for teacher strikes: Mississippi, Alabama, Georgia, Idaho, New Mexico, South Carolina, South Dakota, and Utah on his list.[xcviii] I would go ahead and add Florida, and then the rest of the country.

# MONEY TALKS

Jane McAlevey, an organizer and labor scholar pretty much predicted the teacher strikes in her book *No Shortcuts* published in 2016. In her viewpoint, the pendulum is simply starting to swing back, and "everyone is just done with having no money. There's nowhere to go but up."[xcix]

Money talks...here and in China, as my father would say (it's a saying in Spanish). Let's reiterate some numbers. Miami-Dade County Public Schools runs a $5.2 billion budget. Yes, *billion*. According to a M-DCPS School Board meeting, over 700 administrators at the district are receiving a salary of over $100,000. Then, we don't have money to pay teachers, but there is money to keep the A/C on at my school all day, every day, and to keep it at frigid temperatures (I'm talking below 70 degrees). Most non-school personnel cringe when they step foot in a classroom at M-DCPS. And teachers don't have control over the thermostat. Downtown takes care of that, according to the district mechanics sent over. Lights are on almost all day, and a single custodian is usually in charge of ensuring that all lights are off after all classrooms have been cleaned around 8 or 9 P.M. I wonder what the light bill looks like for the almost 400 schools in the district. Then, there's the food. If I had a penny for every tray of food that is partially, or mostly full, and is thrown out every day in the school cafeteria, I would be a billionaire. I might need to add up all the trays in M-DCPS, but you get the idea. Trays of food are thrown out because the food is tasteless and has been known to cause stomach aches often.

And then there's my favorite "other" senseless ways to waste money. Most recently, my school in Miami Beach had to go through what's called a "name change" because politicians deemed that every school located in Miami Beach needed to actually have that delineated in the name. I remember someone telling me how much these meetings, sign changes, new letterheads etc. would cost, but

I'm almost glad that I don't remember the actual number. So much money is spent on the special programs that have been given grant money from the federal or state government that are of no use to teachers or students. I call this the dog-and-pony show.

Enough complaining. How do we make use of money in a positive way? Obviously, we need to cut the wasteful spending and stop the bleeding, so to speak. We can also bring in private money. I've had friends with MBA's ask me how the private sector can contribute to the public sector with education. I don't know is my short answer. What I do know is that there's enough interest, enough money, and enough intelligence as a human race to be able to merge the public and private sectors to really make changes in education. All we need is coordination, synergy, and unity.

**DISTRICTS IN FLORIDA WOULD RATHER PAY A FINE TO THE STATE IN ORDER TO SUPERSEDE THEIR CLASS SIZE LIMITS - THAN HIRE A TEACHER.
YEP.
IT'S CHEAPER.**

And that's why class size limits aren't really enforced, even though they do exist.

**A RECENT MIAMI HERALD ARTICLE** *SHOWED THAT TEACHERS IN MIAMI-DADE COUNTY CAN ONLY AFFORD THE BOTTOM 9% OF HOUSING.*[c]

# PART IV
# HEAR ME ROAR

## Under Pressure

The pressure is on. A teacher could be a circus performer. Looking for a master juggler??? We found one! Here she is...a teacher. A teacher can multi-task like no other. A teacher can keep track of twenty or so students at a time. If the teacher is a good one, the students will all be learning simultaneously and harmoniously in one room. This requires one eye on the small group that the teacher is teaching, and the other eye on the rest of the groups for behavior enforcement.

Now let's zoom out. When the classroom teacher isn't actually teaching, the teacher gets to grade papers. Let's stop here for a moment. If a teacher isn't departmentalized, then that teacher usually teaches five subjects, which is what I used to teach. This will equate to approximately 900 assignments that need to be graded per quarter (nine grades per subject per student –let's say 20 students to make it easy). There are four quarters, by the way, so there's a total of 3,600 assignments per academic year that need to be graded. Then, these same teachers get to input grades in a computer program, keep track of attendance reports, i-Ready reports (these are weekly), report cards, behavior management, and rewards and incentives for the classroom. There are grade-level meetings, bi-weekly school meetings, copies (lots and lots of copies), meetings with parents, communication with parents via email, newsletter, or phone app. There are binders that must be kept. Binders regarding data about your students, any special accommodations for any of your students that must be tracked, SCAM reports for bad behavior, ESOL levels, information provided at any professional development. There's paper work from the district, the school, and your own classroom that must be signed by each parent, collected, and kept. There's a binder with detailed weekly lesson plans (oh yeah –let's not forget those), pacing guides, materials needed for the actual lessons. There are binders and folders for each student because all student work must be kept for at least a year after the student has left the school. There are binders and folders for emergency plans and substitute plans (yes, you will need to leave these if you plan on getting sick, going to a professional development, or taking a personal day). Once most of the paperwork is taken care of, then the teacher can focus on the beautification of her or his classroom. This will require putting up student work, taking down student work, displaying certain bulletin boards with specific information that is required, incentivizing students, maybe you have time to take pictures of every student, printing them out, paying for them, and then putting them up. Please keep all receipts because teachers need to itemize every expense in order to be reimbursed for anything. Teachers need to make homework packets, plan for test prep, plan pep rallies, and celebrate birthday parties. Are you tired yet? I'll also add that this doesn't include anything *extra*. This doesn't include any committee you may have volunteered for, have been asked to participate in, or agreed to because a colleague or administrator begged you to do. Teachers are patient and usually comply with a smile, generally speaking.

This is school. Most teachers have families that they go home to. I don't know what it's like to then add home juggling to the mix so I won't speak on it. I only have two pets: a dog and a fish.

And now come results. A teacher's students need to show positive results. Every student needs to show growth –lots of growth. It doesn't matter if the student is one or two grade levels behind. It doesn't matter if the child has an undiagnosed learning disability, or a diagnosed learning disability and you don't have support. It doesn't matter if you've never met the parent or if the child doesn't speak English yet. Classroom teachers need to show results on testing and in data reports. Period.

And, finally, teachers are pillars of society. A teacher's job requires an extra dose of ethical behavior, neutrality, and perfectionism. Most recently, in the last couple of years, teachers got to watch presentations and videos on ethics during our bi-weekly school meetings to assist us with grey areas that may be problematic. These were sent by the district who needed to ensure that teachers abide by these high ethical standards. My favorite of these suggestions is to stay *apolitical* on my Facebook feed. Yes, as a teacher, I wouldn't want to seem like I have an incendiary political opinion. It's frowned upon.

I found an interesting article entitled, "Where Do Teachers Get the Most Respect?" The article explains the findings of the 2018 Global Teacher Status Index, a worldwide survey of the general public and educators in 35 countries on the status of the teaching profession around the world. It scored various countries around the world to quantify how educators are respected in relation to other professions. The article suggests that this score determines an educator's overall status in an individual country. In China and Malaysia, the teaching profession is often placed on par with doctors. In Finland, the public aligns teaching with social work. Other countries rank teaching alongside librarians. China scored a 100, giving it the highest score in 2018, which means that teachers are very respected in China. Malaysia scored a 93, the U.S. scored a 39, Argentina scored a 23.6, Israel scored a 6.6, and Brazil scored a 1, sadly, showing their complete disregard for teachers.[ci]

I vote that, until the U.S.'s score doesn't move up to a 100, teachers don't need to meet the ridiculously high standards set in front of them. Once educators are respected enough, paid enough, and heard enough, then and only then, should they be examined enough.

# JUST.
# PILE.
# IT.
# ON.

It seems to be that every few years, or after a bill passes, more and more requirements are piled on to a teacher. For example, in Miami-Dade County, it's mandatory for a teacher to be ESOL- certified. This is not everywhere. It is the case here because there's such a high percentage of ESOL/ELL students, which stands for English for Speakers of Other Languages, or English Language Learners, respectively. This also means that, as a teacher, after spending time and money to get ESOL-certified, you are now expected to teach any ESOL/ELL learner in your classroom. This entails a lot. It means creating separate assessments, or tests, teaching basic language skills, and even more variance in differentiated instruction in general. I've asked myself, is there anything wrong with expanding our knowledge base, as teachers, and growing as professionals? Of course not. But are we paid any more for this extra set of skills? NO.

Let's continue. The newest bill HB887 is requiring that for the 2020-2021 school year, all teachers who teach Reading intervention (*which is all teachers*) must be Reading endorsed.[cii] For most of you who don't know, a Reading endorsement is the equivalent to a master's degree in Reading, according to Miami-Dade County. If you already have a master's degree in Reading, then congratulations because you don't have to worry. If, however, you don't (which is most teachers) please prepare for almost one full year of extra classes to become an "expert" at teaching Reading. This means that after your long workday, you will need to carve out some time to go to class from 5:30 P.M.-9:30 P.M., twice a week for one to two years. Oh, and it won't be easy to get into these classes offered by the school district because thousands of teachers (most of the 18,000 teachers in the district) need to take them. Again, will the state pay any of these over qualified teachers a penny more for their efforts? Nope. We should just be grateful to keep our jobs, I guess.

What about the states that already require a master's degree to teach? Well, those states pay better. Thank you, New York.

And now let's add to that. We now, also, have a requirement to be ESE teachers. ESE stands for "Exceptional Student Education." This can mean either "gifted" students, or students with learning disabilities. An online crash course of approximately 20 hours will deem us certified to teach ESE as well. What does this mean in the classroom? This means that schools don't have to provide ESE teachers, who only specialize in teaching these specialized groups of children, because now a general education teacher gets to handle those issues in the classroom, in addition to her average group. Part of the reason this has come up is because there aren't enough teachers getting certified as ESE teachers any more. The teacher shortage has begun to take effect. Again, are we paid anymore for this new set of skills, or for the added complications in the classroom??? Of course not.

And, if you're wondering why there are more requirements for teachers, at all, I have an answer. There has been a big change in Miami-Dade County in the last five years. Our higher performing students have moved on to charter, magnet, or private schools. This has left public schools with a lot more average to below average students than before. As a result, teachers need different skills in order to teach this student population, which does require some ESE training, and which would benefit from a Reading endorsement, since it teaches teachers more skills to teach Reading successfully. Why is the state requiring all of these extra certifications, specializations, and skills of every single teacher? Well, because they don't have the money to pay extra personnel or resources for these children. They also don't have the money to pay these teachers for these extra skills and for their time. They figure that teachers will want to keep their jobs and will do it anyway.

Ironically, as more skills are required of teachers already in the system, the Florida legislature has simultaneously lowered requirements for new teachers entering the system. The Senate Education committee filed SPB 7070 in February 2019, removing barriers to Florida's teacher certification process and SB 1576, which gives more flexibility to aspiring teachers in taking the FTCE, the test required for a teacher's license.[ciii] Why do I think there is this paradox? Simply because there is a teacher shortage in Florida and across the nation. The strategy seems simple: to attract as many able-bodies as possible, and then cut costs wherever and whenever possible.

At the end of the day, teachers will be necessary no matter what happens. With the present formula in place, good teachers will simply move on to charter or private schools. The leftovers will teach to the poor or ESE population, which leads me to my next thought. Public education has been a pathway out of poverty for families for generations, but that pathway is blocked when schools are unable to offer a decent education. All too often, low-income students end up in schools with the lowest funding, fewest supplies, the least rigorous curriculum, and the oldest facilities and equipment, according to the U.S. Commission on Civil Rights. [civ] Education is key to opportunity and social change. In the present moment, with the present formula, we're fostering a social divide, a greater inequality amongst us, and greater resentments, beginning with our children.

# Inequities amongst teachers

One day I was talking with our school Art teacher, and we started talking about working in the inner city in Miami. She was telling me that she had an Art teacher friend that worked in the inner city and she started sharing about her experiences. She explained how limited her friend felt working there because of all of the Code Reds and shooting scares, and how the students weren't trusted with a pencil or crayon because they get violent. They actually did stab one another with pencils or crayons and so now those were limited over there. My colleague expressed with disappointment how the one good release those students can get from an Art class is limited for them. Imagine that.

The conversation led to the question of why would her friend want to teach there? I mean, teaching is hard enough. Why would you want to teach someplace where you get the added bonus of worrying about drive-by shootings as you get to your car, or you get to worry about a shooter in the vicinity as you fend for your life at your workplace? I mean, is any job worth all that stress? And then we started talking about how these teachers aren't even paid any more money than I am at my "comfortable" school surrounded by multi-million dollar condos. Now how does that make sense?

How does it make sense that an ESE teacher that teaches children with learning disabilities and specialized needs doesn't get paid more? How is it that someone who's willing to put their life at risk, day in and day out, just to get to the workplace doesn't get paid more? How is it that teachers who serve a population that battles drugs, poverty, neglect, drive-by shootings, and single parent families not get paid more? These children have so many unmet needs that a teacher has to fulfill so many different roles for these students. I'm not saying that we need to eradicate our society of poverty or fix all of our societal ills to make things more just, but it is my intention to add awareness to what teachers do, how they sacrifice, and how their needs aren't being met.

My colleague and I then applied the conversation to our own school and the disparity between teachers at our school. She wondered how it was possible that she was on the same pay scale and got paid the same amount as a classroom teacher, when she had a lot fewer demands as a special area teacher. She shared with me how, technically, she didn't have to teach on Wednesdays, and yet she would help out where they needed teachers or proctors instead, out of the generosity of her heart. We talked about the heaviness of being a classroom teacher, of having to be involved in everything regarding your students, and how tiresome it is to run the ship constantly. We talked about how these disparities just don't make sense.

I would often discuss with my family why I stayed a "testing teacher," even though it's more work and more demands for the same pay (a testing teacher in elementary schools means $3^{rd}$-$5^{th}$ grade). I did it only because I loved my $3^{rd}$ grade team so much. As a testing teacher, I had more work than if I were a 1st grade or 2nd grade teacher, academically speaking. (I do want to clarify, however, that I'm a firm believer that the younger the students are, the harder the job is for a teacher). Having clarified my opinion, as a testing teacher you have very real added pressure with tests, and usually those tests bring more grading and work. Why did I decide to continue at this grade level when it's more work for the same pay? I did it because I loved the colleagues who I worked with and who added value to my life, as opposed to my paycheck. So, I stayed.

How do we even out the playing field amongst teachers? The way I see it, either teachers agree to different salaries based on actual accountable responsibilities and criteria, or we divide and conquer as a school. Could there be a system set up whereby a teacher can "pick up" extra duties not assigned to her or his workload, in order to earn extra pay? What's possible? Can teachers, voluntarily, agree to divide and conquer the work at each school, on a school-by-school basis?

## Things Just Don't Make Sense in the Microcosm

When my colleague and friend, Roxanne, first moved down from Orlando, Florida (Orange County– a different county) she would knock on my classroom door to ask me about where to find certain resources. She was looking for bouncy chairs for children with ADHD, audio books, specific workbooks, manipulatives, and the list went on and on. I would smile and respond, honestly, that I had never heard of these things, or that I had no idea what she was talking about. The only thing I could suggest was that she could try to buy these items for her students with her annual stipend for the classroom. I couldn't have foreseen that this would become a running joke between us, as we would refer to the "resource room." It was the fictional place where you could find everything you could possibly need or want for your classroom. Whenever we found ourselves short on resources or in a situation where our needs weren't met, we would declare aloud that all we needed to do was visit the "resource room." We would chuckle every time, and then joke with the new teachers, as we suggested that they go to the magical "resource room" to find their supplies.

Unfortunately for the public school system, there most often isn't a "resource room." As a matter of fact, there is NO room where you can find solutions to your problems; moreover, even when you think a solution is being given to your problem, it's usually met with another problem. There is a lot of incompetence going around in the system.

Let me give you a simple example. One day my classroom was "gifted" a Promethean board by the district. This is a big, electronic board that is connected to your computer, which basically has replaced the chalkboard, and then white board, that was used for many generations. It's the latest technology used in the district where you can pull up anything that you see on your computer for your students, and then write on it with a magic pen (which is very cool), amongst other things.

Now, before this state-of-the-art Promethean board, I had the older, clunkier version of this board called the SMART board. It worked very well and I loved it. It was the same thing, but just an older version. I want to be clear that I was not given a choice about the Promethean board. I was absent one day, and the next day, it was there. I didn't ask for it, and I also didn't know it would be installed in my room because the school system doesn't have time for things like that. I walked into my room that morning and my boards and things had been shifted. Boom. I thought, "lucky me...I get one." I was uncertain about how I felt about it, as I picked up the trash and the pieces of my bulletin board that had been left strewn around the classroom.

It soon dawned on me that I didn't know anything about this board, including how to turn it on. My students wound up telling me that they knew how to turn it on and where the remote and "magic pen" was located. At least it seemed like *they* had gotten a very minor tutorial while I was gone. As a couple of days went by, no one could tell me how to *actually* use it. Finally, I complained to the IT guy, who would come around every so often. I complained about the difficulties of teaching Math, when I couldn't pull up the book on the board, as my students were used to seeing. I'm pretty sure my arms were flailing as I explained this fact. As the young, sweet, competent man that he was, he decided to "look up" some information on this board in order to help me out.

It turns out that this IT guy looked for a basic tutorial, and then came by a week later to teach me how to use the basics. Before this, though, our full-time, school IT guy had to wipe my computer clean to upload the latest version of Windows onto my computer, in order to even use the Promethean board. High-tech technology requires high-tech technology, he explained. After having it wiped, both men admitted that my computer was now going to have problems given that it was ancient (about 15 years old), and really couldn't support such high-tech technology very well. Great. Now my computer was slow.

I then came to find out that I was extremely lucky to have the young IT guy come teach me the tutorial because teachers weren't getting a tutorial until probably the summer time. I got my Promethean board in October. I thought to myself, why would you implement something expensive that no one knows how to use and then give a tutorial on it eight months later? To add injury to insult, I was given a remote control for the volume on the Promethean, but unfortunately, this fancy remote requires a small and fancy battery, which doesn't come with the board. I had a choice. I could now go hunting to buy this battery and pay for it myself, or I could just adjust to getting on a chair every time I needed a volume change. I chose the latter.

In conclusion, I was left with a new board that I never asked for, that I didn't know how to use, and that I wouldn't be taught how to use for another eight months. And I would now have to stand on a chair every time I wanted to turn on the volume on my computer because the remote control that controls it, doesn't work. And, finally, my computer was using a version of Windows that it couldn't support, and it would now be so slow that I would need to have it repaired, as it was actually detracting from my teaching time.

And this is just one example of how things work in the public school system. In the life-coaching world, it is said that the way you do one thing, is the way you do everything. In my experience, this rings true every time. In the public school system, *everything* is done in a way that doesn't make sense.

# Testing

As a testing teacher, I can speak to the demands of state testing. At my final Open House, I had parents ask me why I'm expecting the children to be able to decipher and break up such complicated texts. I told them that, while I teach great test-taking skills, and skills in general that are good to know, it wasn't my decision to teach them this at the age of eight. I explained to these parents that teachers don't choose the test they will be judged by; instead, they should turn their attention to their local politicians and the governor of the state. This was met with some laughs, and side jokes.

As any testing teacher will tell you, the test matters. It matters a lot. Whether you're ok with it or not, the scores that your students achieve will be perused closely and your results will be analyzed. Did enough students pass the test? Did the students show growth, academically speaking? How much growth? Did the majority grow? For the ones that didn't grow, WHY didn't they grow? And, by the way, you will be asked to show paperwork in response to why they didn't grow enough. Teachers are judged by these scores because of the way the system is set up to work in each state. Of course, it's not because your administration is evil or hates you, but because they also have a job to do, just like everyone down the chain of command.

Where is the starting point of state testing, you ask? The starting point is with the person who chooses the state test, i.e. the Governor. Depending on how challenging or fair the test is, this one choice dictates a lot. The next big decision is the way in which the state decides how to rank schools based on this test. In Florida, the grading system is A through F. An "A" school is excellent and by the time a school enters a "D" or "F" status, then the state is intervening with their own system to try and "save" the school. The formula for ranking a school gets very complicated, and can probably only be explained by a select few in the state. No, I'm not kidding. It's been joked about and talked about by several administrators in Miami-Dade County.

As a result, the state test matters a lot for each school. Just as every teacher is judged by the scores of her or his students, the school is judged by the scores of its students. The school will be ranked somewhere between an A and an F, and this will greatly impact the school and the administration. What does this mean then in the day-to-day? It means that from Day 1 of the school year, teachers are analyzing how they're going to structure their routines, homework, and classwork because it needs to be beneficial towards the test. Let me give a real-life example. If grammar is heavy on the state test, then logically speaking, every teacher should focus on a lot of grammar over the course of the school year. Is grammar important? Sure. So are many other things. If the test didn't focus on grammar, then would this teacher or grade level place as much focus and emphasis on grammar? Probably not. This is what we call "teaching to the test." It doesn't mean that educators are teaching useless content. It just means that educators will prioritize and focus on content that will also assist the students at the end-of-the-year state test. After all, the teacher doesn't want the students to fail for various reasons: a student retention means that a student has to go through that on an emotional and psychological level, it looks bad for the teacher and her or his scores, and finally, it looks bad upon the school, which is then pestered by the district, which goes all the way up to the state level.

What bothers me the most about state testing, however, is the pressure inflicted upon THE STUDENTS! It has left a bitter taste in my mouth. The fear that I've seen in some of their eyes as I pass out practice tests and then the REAL test, one-by-one, has me look within. What message are we sending to these children? Based on what I've seen, we're sending the message that many of them are already "failing." Are they failing at life, possibly? At age eight? What should they look forward to then? I don't even ask myself if it's unfair that they feel this pressure. *Of course it's unfair*! Again, they're eight. I've seen heartfelt tears of disappointment and fear in some of these children that has been heart-wrenching. I've seen children vomit from the nerves on testing day, which is also unfair. For what? What does this state test prove to them? To us? To society, at large? Who's winning in this scenario?

And I want to be clear that I don't have a vendetta against tests. Tests are necessary. It's necessary to assess a student to see what he or she has learned. It's necessary to understand where they are presently, in order to take them to where they are going. There is a huge impact, however, in what test you choose and what you use it for. Since I taught the 3rd grade, I'll focus on it. Third grade is a retention year along with 7th and 11th grades. In the 3rd grade, the state test is supposed to determine if the students are reading well enough or not. Of course, it's important to know if a student is reading at level or, if not, how far below the student is in order to keep them growing as readers. The problem comes in, though, when all of this responsibility falls upon the 3rd grade teachers. In my viewpoint, and the viewpoint of many other teachers, the testing done at the end of the year should determine if a child should move on or be retained that year. Retention shouldn't just be enforced in the 3rd grade in elementary school.

And a student shouldn't just be retained for reading. A child's level for reading and math during these early years should be assessed at the end of every year, and a child shouldn't move on unless she or he has mastered these necessary skills every year. Otherwise, the system ends up with students who can read well enough, but are two or three levels behind in math and, possibly, other subjects. The building blocks of learning are in elementary school and reading and math skills need to be mastered at this level.

Retention shouldn't be a shameful subject either. If we allow for and use retention at every grade level, then the taboo behind it will be dissolved. Parents and students should understand that certain skills need to be mastered in order to move on. Period. It will be much better for that student to master those skills one year later, as opposed to just getting passed on and ignored year after year, with years full of academic Fs. Getting straight Fs year after year is what is demoralizing for students.

And, finally, of course the test matters. It should be a fair test. Simple. One for reading and one for math. Sure, some of the topics can incorporate science or social studies topics as well. The test shouldn't be designed to stump them. If I told you what some of my

3rd grade students needed to read about in some of these passages of the FSA (Florida Standards Assessment), you wouldn't believe me. Again, what does an eight-year old really understand about curing meat? Or about Chinese dynasties? Or about some complicated scientific process? The test doesn't need to be so hard in order to assess a child's reading level.

I will share a fun fact. The FSA test came to Florida when Governor Rick Scott and his advisors chose it. That test had been used or tested in Utah. The Governor paid millions of dollars for this random test to come to Florida. And then guess what? More than half of the students tested in Utah failed, and eventually the state dumped it.[cv] And so why did we keep it?

# PART V
# SOME TRUTHS

# The Case For ADD or ADHD

I get a lot of questions about ADD and ADHD. Why does it happen? Is it hereditary? Is it nature or nurture? Do you find that it's more common now than before? Is it because of the video games? Do you recommend medication for it?

This topic is complicated, but I want to address it from a teacher's standpoint because I feel that it will support others. I also want to start by reminding you that I'm not a psychologist, psychiatrist, or doctor who has a medical opinion. My opinion is based solely on my experience as a teacher and on what I've seen in the classroom.

First and foremost, ADD and ADHD are not too different. A child showing symptoms of ADD requires some extra attention in the classroom and some extra "tools." This child learns differently; in short spurts. This child needs movement, a change of scenery often, more experiential learning, and a blank wall in front of them when doing homework or taking a test. They are prone to distractions and will need frequent redirection. A child with ADD doesn't learn less than an average child; a child with ADD learns *differently*. I have found that once parents acknowledge the symptoms and learn these tools to improve performance, the child benefits greatly. Most importantly, you begin to teach the child what works for them and what doesn't work. By continuously using these tools with the child, you allow for them to integrate the tools and, as they mature, they can take these tools with ease into adulthood.

The biggest difference between a child with ADD and ADHD is the "hyper" component (this is where the "H" comes in). ADHD is also less common and the characteristics are more intense. As a teacher, you can spot a child with ADHD a mile away, once you have a few years of experience. These students are hyper, move around a lot, have trouble maintaining focus, and usually like to call attention. These children tap into fun and play, and can often express love or feelings easily. They are often better in touch with themselves than an average child. They also tend to be more emotional than average and can have outbursts. And of course, I want to clarify that every child who exhibits symptoms of ADHD or ADD is unique, as every human is, and some cases are more extreme than others.

What does a child exhibiting symptoms of ADHD look like in a classroom? Well…they are the centerpiece of your room. They are the couch in the living room. You can't miss them and your eye will naturally gravitate towards them! They have VIP status whether you gave it to them or not, and they will consume most of your day and most of your school year for that matter. A child with ADHD is outgoing, extroverted, and will be the center of attention whether for better or worse. Their playfulness will get their classmates' attention, and their outbursts will as well. It is impossible to miss them. In a classroom, they can run amuck and they can anger their classmates, as quickly as they can inspire a game of tag inside the classroom. They are difficult to "manage" in a classroom to say the least.

A child with ADHD also has hyper focus, which means that when this child is engaged in something that they truly like, this child will become completely engrossed in the project in front of them until it's completed. For this reason, psychologists and social workers will recommend that you give this child many tasks and "special" rules in order to keep them engaged. By "special" rules I mean rules that help keep the child on track and are individualized for them. Now, the difficulty for the teacher or parent lies in creating an endless list of tasks for the child, and following through with them, in order to prevent the child from getting bored and into trouble. If you've ever heard the saying, "idle hands are the devil's workshop," you'll appreciate it more when in the presence of a child with ADHD. You want to make sure they're not idle!

For this reason, coming up with those tasks and projects while managing another 20 children (on average) becomes difficult for a teacher on a daily basis. This leaves the teacher with a very unruly, and hard to handle student, who is usually highly disruptive to the classroom environment and to classroom management. For a parent or a tutor, a one-on-one interaction with a child who exhibits ADHD is usually very positive because they tend to be more mature, more personable, and can connect easily to others. In the classroom, though, this child will be a lot of work, and will likely be the "star" of the teacher's school year. A good day in the classroom will mean peace and gratitude. A bad day in the classroom will leave the teacher feeling drained and upset.

How do I feel about medication for children who exhibit these symptoms, you ask? Well, I have seen extreme differences when a child is medicated vs. not medicated and I've also seen cases where the payoff is questionable. When a child is on medication, and the medication has a positive influence, then the child can slow down and focus much better on their average tasks in the classroom. They usually become a lot more manageable and perform better. When the medication doesn't sit well with a child, then the child becomes more emotionally volatile and/or sedentary, in my experience. By emotionally volatile, I mean to say that the child can transition from sadness, to anger, to joy very quickly and suddenly. By sedentary, I mean that I've seen children become indifferent to everything and their emotions seem depressed. I've wondered how much of an impact it's having on subduing their emotions or their daily experience of life. Of course, I don't like it when either of these effects happen. As a teacher, I *can* tell you that when a child isn't medicated and it's an extreme case, which means that the child is extremely ADD or ADHD, then the child should try medication to see how it works. It simply is too hard for that child to perform in an average school setting and it demands too much energy from that teacher. In my opinion, the parents must do their own cost/benefit analysis when it comes to medication for their child, as every child is unique and every child may experience different symptoms and outcomes. Generally speaking, I believe that medication should only be used in extreme cases where it becomes difficult for the child to perform in an average setting.

Now that we see cases of ADD/ADHD and learning disabilities regularly in the school system, and we can actually put a name to the condition or disability and talk about it, now what? How do we best service these children? They will soon be a part of our workforce and society. How can we help them to be functional and successful members of society? The short answer is by giving them tools. Tools that will help them emotionally, and their functioning in the classroom and in life. We need social workers, psychologists, and *trained* teachers for this mission. We also need a safe space for these children to learn these tools. It's impossible for them to learn these tools in the present public school environment. There's too many demands, too little assistance, and too much ignorance on the subject. These groups of children need to be pulled out of the classroom by mental health professionals for part of the day in order to be trained, or should be in a separate classroom until these tools are learned. After this work has been done, they can be introduced into a more traditional classroom and school setting with the rules and norms that come with it. This, of course, is a luxury in the eyes of education in the present moment. We barely have enough teachers and support staff to teach in a rigid, traditional environment that comes with a lot of rules and norms.

We should provide support for two imperative reasons. The first reason may seem unfair, but it really isn't…to conserve teachers. With high needs like what I've described in the classroom, teachers are worn out and worn thin by the end of the year. With the way the system is set up, teachers are worn, year after year, after year and it causes breakdowns and indifference for teachers. By actually supporting these children, you also provide support to their amazing teachers who will not be as drained by the end of the year. Teachers will last longer in the profession if we conserve their energy in situations as described above. And if that's not enough of a reason for you, then look at it economically. The state will save more money by keeping experienced teachers in the profession; meaning that it will lose less money by needing to hire new or inexperienced teachers who will not be able to perform as well as the one that burned out due to high output. Hiring and training new teachers is expensive just like in any business model. I don't have a degree in business, but I believe it's always or usually better to retain experienced and skilled workers in the field.

And the second reason that we should provide support to these groups of children is for the *common good*. Yes, I had to say it. If we can provide support services for children that need it, then, we are in turn providing support for our communities and society. Many of these children grow up with the grave misconception that they're dumb or that they can't learn because all they saw were Fs on their report cards. Not only is this false, damaging, and soul-wrenching, but it's also untrue. Their sometimes obsessive and intense nature allows for a drive that is hard to quench and they become hyper-focused on whatever result they desire. Who doesn't want an employee who's willing to leave it all on the table when inspired? Who doesn't want an employee who's willing to do whatever it takes to make it to the goal? *Everyone* wants this employee!

If we don't offer support or impart the knowledge we have, then many of these children wind up wandering or "lost" because they truly believe that they can't learn or that school isn't for them. Society, as a whole, loses out on their potential and, moreover, they're not successful at adapting to society's rules, which also causes problems. Let's continue down the rabbit hole. Society ends up paying a price when groups of children who are "bad" at school, through no fault of their own, have a higher likelihood to land in jail or depend on societal hand-outs. Everyone is entitled to help at some point or many points in their life, but it's completely unnecessary for this group of actually gifted, hyper-focused children to end up with handicaps such as these. I'm saying that I would rather provide less money to build jail cells and more money on education to help curb these souls from ending up in jail in the first place. Time and time again, teachers, being well aware of society's ills, can identify early on the children that can't read well, or have a learning disability, that will probably end up taking a difficult or wrong path. All because no one took the time to teach them how to read or do math well. Of course, often times these children don't come from comfortable, secure households. Sometimes their only advocate is the teachers. Teachers see societal ills, firsthand, when they're young and small. We see the possibility in these young souls…both the good and the bad. We see it all and we wish someone would just listen to us.

# Mental Health

What does it mean to have a social worker and counselor on campus? Well, it means you have support when your student is having emotional issues or is struggling with something from home, which by the way, is often. Sometimes we forget that in school we teach the whole child. This means that we can't compartmentalize a child. We can't ask him or her to be a sole academic creature. If the child-student is going through some difficult emotional time at school or at home, or both, it will affect this child. As I've said before, teachers are as much "therapists," as they are academic teachers.

And so in comes the social worker. What is a social worker exactly? A social worker is defined as "a person who works for the social services or for a private organization providing help and support for people who need it."[cvi] In schools, these are professionally trained people who assist children with their emotional needs. They provide short counseling sessions, evaluate the child, teach coping skills, keep a record of the child's progress, and provide home visits if necessary.

Teachers are grateful for social workers because they will come into your classroom, if you have a child with emotional issues, and take them for a short amount of time and be helpful to them. Now let's keep in mind that a child that has been "flagged" for a social worker is likely to have serious behavioral or emotional issues. This means that most teachers won't have contact with a social worker, unless they have a "problematic" child on their hands.

Now...what's the problem with social workers? None. Only that there aren't enough of them and there isn't enough money being pumped into this need. At my small school of approximately 500 students, there were usually two social workers on campus. One of them could only come once a week, which meant that she had to see all of her cases, in one day, for a school of 500. The other social worker was available to see cases about three times per week. There is no way that any one, or barely two, social workers can actually service this many students. The ratio is preposterous.

This sad ratio actually applies to every aspect of health and mental health in schools. In March 2019, the American Civil Liberties Union found some scary numbers: [cvii]

- 444:1 the student to counselor ratio across the U.S. (students are in schools with police but no counselor, nurse, psychologist, or social worker

- 1.7 million students with no counselors

- 3 million students with no nurses

- 6 million students with no school psychologists

- 10 million students with no social workers

Schools have become essentially the de facto mental health system for students, which may be jarring to many educators, district leaders, and parents. [cviii] At this point, I want to remind you that I've only worked at the elementary level and that the emotional/behavioral issues aren't that grand, yet. Imagine what the needs are at middle schools, and high schools. Kathy Reamy, a school counselor who also chairs the NEA School Counselor Caucus, says that she's "had more students this year [2018] hospitalized for anxiety, depression, and other mental-health issues than ever." In her opinion, "there's just so much going on in this day and age, the pressure to fit in, the pressure to achieve, the pressure of social media." [cix] Schools have become a "pressure cooker" for students and staff, and student and teacher stress feed off each other. Teachers need adequate support and resources to battle burnout and alleviate stress in the classroom, which they're clearly not getting, presently. 93% of elementary school teachers report they are "highly stressed."

The facts speak for themselves: [cx]

- **10 million**: mental health issues affect 1 in 5 students, ages 13-18. **That's approximately 10 million public school students across the U.S. who need professional help**

- **11% of youth have a mood disorder such as depression, anxiety, or bipolar disorder. 10% have a behavior or conduct disorder. 8% have an anxiety disorder**

- **½ of mental health disorders begin before age 14 and ¾ before age 24**

- Treatment helps: studies show **81% of teens with anxiety, 71% of teens with depression, and 85% of teens with ADHD get better with treatment**

- **70% of students with a mental health disorder do not receive adequate treatment**

- Programs help: **School-based education and anti-stigma programs improve mental health attitudes by 68%**

The growing crisis around students' mental health, and the scarcity of available care, has long been a concern of educators and health professionals. Interest from lawmakers, however, is a relatively new trend, sparked primarily by the onslaught of mass shootings. After the Marjory Stoneman Douglas High School shooting in February 2018, in Parkland, Florida, there's been a call for more mental health counseling in Florida. Obvious, no? Senate Bill 7026 has allocated approximately $6.2 million to Miami-Dade County Public Schools for the establishment or expansion of mental health services. The Senate bill now *requires* the County to expand or establish mental health services. As a result, Superintendent Alberto Carvalho has spearheaded the newly minted Mental Health Department at Miami-Dade County Public Schools. The purpose of the Mental Health Department is to coordinate and facilitate services between schools and community agencies and ensure students who are referred for mental health care and treatment are accessing services.[cxi]

The establishment of this department in 2018 is a step in the right direction. It's just a shame that it took one of the largest school shootings, to date, to spur it. And, by the way, Miami-Dade County Public Schools has the highest rate of Baker Acts in the state. If you don't know, a Baker Act is the Florida law that allows people with mental illnesses to be held involuntarily for up to 72 hours in a mental health treatment facility if they meet certain criteria. Yes, there are many elementary, middle, and high school students that meet this criteria and are taken by law enforcement during school hours, in case you didn't know.

There needs to be a call for mental health work, nationwide, if we want to curb the frequency of school shootings. School shooters are children with serious emotional needs who have been neglected *for a long time*. These behaviors don't show up overnight. Ask any teacher. We see behaviors that should be flagged at an early age. These children have a lack of coping mechanisms, and often, a dysfunctional home life. The neglect begins at home, and then the children fall through the cracks in the school system, which shouldn't be surprising given the lack of resources. Sometimes it should be obvious to parents, but we can't rely on good parenting. And so we have situations where these children, who are suffering, may opt for the trending mass shooting or suicide. It's a taboo subject that few people want to talk about it, but pulling the wool over our eyes isn't helping anybody. And much less our children.

Much of the national conversation has been inherently reactive, focusing on "crisis response," in particular to school shootings, rather than a systematic approach to helping students with their mental health needs. What schools really need is early identification, prevention, and routine care. Joe O'Callaghan, the head of Stamford Public Schools social work department in Connecticut, helped lead a district-wide effort to overhaul Stamford Public School's mental health program after three students from three different high schools took their own lives in 2014. In his opinion, the goal is to create a self-sustaining, in-house program. In a "whole-school program, everybody needs to be relating to and engaging with each other over students who are experiencing difficult things in their lives." [cxii]

Despite the obvious return on investment, comprehensive mental health programs are still only scattered across the country. Schools are hiring personnel to help keep students safe, but they're not bringing in counselors. Instead, a lot of money is being spent on enforcement and discipline —even though much of the evidence points to this not working.

**With everything you now know about teachers and how much they GIVE, are you really going to ask them to consider carrying a gun to school??? Seriously?**

# Guns

In March 2018, the National Education Association (NEA) surveyed 1,000 NEA members nationwide (a.k.a teachers) and asked their opinions about arming teachers. 74% of these educators opposed arming teachers, 82% wouldn't carry a gun in school, 63% of gun-owning NEA members would not agree to be armed in school, 67% say arming teachers would make schools less safe, and 60% worry there could be a mass shooting in their school.[cxiii] *Yes, teachers now think about, and actually worry, about school shootings at their schools.* They think about their own lives, and what they would do, if faced with the lives of their students in their hands.

And what about the students? The Pew Research Center conducted a survey two months after the Parkland shooting which showed that 57% of U.S. teenagers are worried that a shooting could take place at their own school. 1 in 4 are "very worried" about the chance of a school shooting. Since the historic shooting at Columbine High School in April of 1999, more than 187,000 U.S. students have been exposed to gun violence in school. Again, according to the survey, 7 in 10 educators said arming school personnel would be ineffective at preventing gun violence in schools and two-thirds said they would feel less safe if school personnel were armed. [cxiv]

And yet, in May 2019, the Florida state legislature voted to allow teachers to carry guns at school despite opposition from many school districts.[cxv] What, exactly, this may look like is difficult to predict, at best; however, I do expect that the school district will continue to oppose any action towards this result, as well as, the union.

With that being said, teachers get a frequent reminder about school shootings and the actions they might be forced to take. A school's monthly practice fire drill, and every so often tornado drill, has now been overshadowed by the Code Yellow(s), Code Red(s), and Active Shooter Drills. These are tons of fun. Teachers and students get to practice moving quickly to a corner of the classroom that is shielded from any window, and huddle. Lights must be turned off, the door must be checked to ensure it's locked, any children in the hallway must be rushed inside, and any window on the door must be covered. We all need to act very quickly, in a matter of a few minutes, to supposedly ensure our safety. Invariably, at the elementary level at least, a teacher will have scared students on the verge of tears, or others who are battling the seriousness of the matter with jokes. Then there are those who ask me, with a blank face, if we will actually survive if there is a real shooter. "Shouldn't we move around instead of staying in one spot?", a few would ask. My last year of teaching, I would treat these drills with indifference and stay as neutral as possible. I would tell my students not to worry about it because it won't happen to them. I preferred to crush any idea of this ever actually happening to myself, my colleagues, or any of my students because I simply can't tolerate the idea of it. The idea of having to fend for my life, the lives of my students, or the lives of my colleagues is unbearable to me. Last I checked, I signed up to improve the lives of children by teaching them everything I know. Last I checked, I have trouble killing an insect. Last I checked, I hate guns. Last I checked, I did not enroll to be a martyr. Last I checked, I didn't register with the army nor sign up to volunteer at any warfront. So what the hell happened?

# PART VI
# WE CAN CREATE SOMETHING NEW FOR OUR CHILDREN

# YOU CAN TEACH A CHILD ANYTHING

For years, I have been meditating. And as my personal practice became stronger, I decided to impart the gift of meditation to my classroom my last few years of teaching. After some practice, I would always reach the point where the classroom was doing it daily and consistently. In the beginning, it's always a bit strange for the children, and I always got some whining about it. As we progressed through it, I learned that interruptions were common, as custodians, students, or other teachers would walk in the room as we would meditate for a few minutes. When I complained to a friend of mine about the interruptions, he suggested that I make a sign. I made a blue sign that informed visitors that we were meditating, and requested that they please wait until we were done. Pretty soon, as I became more comfortable with the whole meditation "thing," the interruptions mysteriously stopped.

We began with three minutes. I would explain to the children that meditation is stopping our fingers from moving, stopping action, and just being. I explained to them that we're trying to stop the mind, too, and that I wanted them to notice that these things that we think are thoughts, and that we actually have control over them. I would explain that they are like clouds moving through us and that we get to watch them, observe them, and then let them go. I would usually use great meditation apps like Calm or Insight Timer, in order to listen to nature sounds such as a rainstorm, water dripping into a fountain, or ocean waves breaking onto the shore. The kids loved these and would ponder quietly which sound I would choose for the day.

My first year, after meditating a few times per week for a few weeks, my girls in the class asked me if we could meditate every day. It was as simple as that. My first reaction was, are they being serious? I only had to think about it for a split second before I agreed. At the time, it was the end of the $2^{nd}$ quarter, and we would be entering test prep season soon so I was a little hesitant about the time commitment. I thought to myself, however, how great it would be if we actually *did* meditate daily, and I figured anyone could give up three minutes of their life –even a teacher.

And so slowly we started getting used to three minutes…and eventually the three minutes started to feel a little short and I started noticing how most of my students actually did stop for those few minutes –even my students with ADHD symptoms. It wasn't every time and it wasn't perfect, but it was a lot, and it was pretty good. *I* also started enjoying my meditation time with them and so I started to increase our time to five minutes on certain days when I needed more of a breather. I started without telling them. And eventually I told them that we were meditating for five whole minutes and I realized that I got very little resistance. After about three months of meditating, I discovered this wonderful feature on this app that provided free guided meditations that were very simple and appropriate to follow. I also discovered that they were a perfect 10 minutes, which at this point, I was curious about for my students. And so they started meditating for 10 minutes about twice per week! Again, even my students with ADHD symptoms could respect our time enough to sit quietly and be still, or mostly still, for these 10 minutes.

What did I learn that I already intuitively knew before? That you can teach a child anything!!!! I'd been saying for some time that I know, as a teacher, that you can teach a child anything. You can teach a child to LOVE, to HATE, to be peace, to be war, to be strong, to be wicked, to be kind, to be selfish. You can teach them to build walls or to bring them down. You can teach a child to build guns or to build peace. You can train them to do anything because all they do is mimic the adults in front of them. It's obvious. Babies learn to speak by mimicking their parents. Children learn how to live by mimicking their parents and their parents' behavior – for better or worse. There is an awful lot of responsibility when being around children.

What did I learn that I didn't know before? I learned that meditation allowed for my kids to play peacefully together. That was the one big change for my class. I also learned that they didn't really need toys anymore either. They could go out to a field and to monkey bars during recess and just enjoy themselves while playing together. They would use their imagination more, and play tag, and run and chase each other, joyfully, with very little conflict. Through meditation, I felt that the barriers between them came down. Differences dissolved. Joy ran through them more easily, rapidly, and often. This isn't to say that I didn't have conflicts for the rest of the year. There's always conflict, but it definitely lessened. Alongside meditation, I've taught my students to speak up and out when they don't like something, when someone is mean to them, and to talk about things, first, in order to resolve conflict. I've taught them to express themselves, to express their grievances, and to listen to the other person. I've also taught them to be accountable –to own their fault in things, or to question how they could've done something better. These habits that I implemented my last few years in the classroom greatly impacted my students in a positive way. It helped the students who didn't seem like they could be helped. And, as a result, I always ended the academic year with a very peaceful, and joyful class. I'm very proud that I've taught my students about emotional intelligence. If that's the only thing they remember or take with them when they walked out of my classroom, I've done an incredible job already.

I've had students who fail every test. I've had students who can barely spell their name. You can call it a learning disability, bad parenting, the result of ADHD or ADD or dyslexia. It doesn't matter. The cause doesn't matter. The point is that every child matters. Every child deserves to learn. And every child needs to understand that we all serve a purpose on this earth. Some will spell very well, some will read very well, some will create new things, some will improve other systems, some will discover, and others will be the support for new businesses. Every child serves a purpose just as every person in society does too. And we are constantly in flux. Our purpose will change consistently.

# A.I.

As we're on the brink of a new decade in our human history, I can't help but wonder if a robot can replace a teacher. Initially, I thought absolutely not. When I asked my 80-something- year-old father who loves sci-fi, he said "of course." This got me wondering. Was I being short-sighted?

As a teacher, you're on the front lines to people's daily lives. This includes heartache, death, divorce, births, everything that we, as humans, experience. Half of the time we're academic teachers and the other half, we're social workers, therapists and psychologists. What is impacting a child in his or her life will impact a child in the classroom. As a teacher, one becomes adept at understanding the child's home life quickly and the impact that it has on him or her.

Given this reality, I have come to the conclusion that a computer or robot will need a large amount of E.Q., or emotional intelligence, in order to replace a teacher. This is assuming that the structure of education remains the same, as in students are dropped off at a separate location for 7-8 hours a day with caregivers and teachers. The robot or computer teacher will need to have algorithms for plan Bs, for different styles of learning, different needs, and most importantly, empathy and understanding of a child's emotional makeup in order to help them navigate through it. If society returns to a home schooling structure, or children become able to learn all academic skills from a computer, then we may not need robots with E.Q. The point I'm trying to make is that a robot, or A.I., will never be able to synthesize all of that information, feeling, emotion, intuition, and compassion without *a lot* of emotional intelligence.

I asked a gifted student of mine in the 4th grade what he thought about robots as teachers. I expected him to like the idea given his appreciation and love of technology and video games. His commentary made me smile. He said, confidently, that it could never work. He said it would be so hard to take a robot seriously. He mimicked a robotic voice telling someone that he was angry. He joked and said that no one would take that "teacher" seriously. He asked me, "how could you even tell if the teacher was mad?" There wouldn't be any emotion. And that would lead children to simply make fun of these robots, he stated. I thought that his grasp of emotional intelligence being necessary in a teacher was thoughtful and beyond his years, which was no surprise to me. I was, however, a little surprised by his answer.

And so, until that day, if that day ever comes, we'll rely on one human superhero to do it all. Because teachers are super humans.

I'll never forget the day I went to yet *another* professional development at some faraway, random location and overheard a fellow teacher's phone conversation during one of our bathroom breaks. He had called his school because he suddenly remembered that one of his students wasn't allowed to go to P.E. due to an injury. He had forgotten to jot that note down in his lesson plans for the substitute, and was worried that the child would forget.

I immediately envisioned my detailed substitute lesson plans, with all of the post-its attached to it, and writing on the edges of it with last-minute notes. As a teacher, away from your classroom, for usually some humdrum professional development class on how to improve some aspect of your teaching, you want to minimize the amount of fires there might be for the substitute. This means that you must leave very detailed notes. Usually there's a few reasons for this. First of all, it's good to be kind to the poor substitute teacher that also isn't getting paid enough and just trying the best she or he can. Second, minimizing fires that need to be put out means that your classroom is in less disarray when you return the next morning. And, finally, you definitely want to avoid any phone calls from administration about some problem that needed to be resolved while you were away.

As I thought about the typed, single-spaced, highly detailed pages of instruction that I neatly left on my desk the day before, I wondered, how many other professions require that level of nurture and commitment? How many other professions require you to be a "professional parent?" How many others would ever understand or appreciate the level of commitment, kindness, concern, and dedication that this young, black male teacher embodied on the phone call in front of me?

Would or *could* a robot remember to make that phone call?

And, finally, A.I may be able to teach your children but it will never be able to give them the love that they need from a teacher.

# A New Era of Teaching

What do you teach a child in the era of Google? I've been approached by many adults asking me this question, which is a good one. How does education calibrate itself in a new age of technology? In an age where most of society has a computer in their pocket most of the time?

I do come across these thoughts fairly often. I stare at the huge collection of dictionaries and thesauruses around the school and ask myself, what to do with these? Is it worth teaching a student how to use a dictionary? They can access any dictionary or thesaurus on their phone and they don't need to know how to find a word alphabetically. They just type in the word. What about being able to alphabetize well, I wonder? How much does that matter?

What do I do with all of these extra books and made-up resources of old text? Should I make these resources the focal point or should I encourage the students to use their online library programs, instead? These programs are cool to ME! I wish I had an extensive online library where the illustrations were top-notch and I could follow along while listening to an exciting story. The students get to read about all sorts of fiction, including comic-style and fantasy books. Most of the time, I would favor that the students got more time for the online libraries. And why not? Their eyes light up when I tell them they can use those programs for a half hour. And isn't that the point of reading? To get to a point where a child is excited to read a story??? Absolutely.

And so...to get back to the question...what should the approach be to teach these I'm-not-sure-what-they're-going-to-be-called-post-millenials? As a teacher, I think the approach needs to be one of inspiration. **We need to inspire this current-and-future generations to want to learn, to want to find out, to want to know how something works or why something is. Then we need to teach them how to find out the answers. And then we need to teach them how to work together because we all know that**

**success is not a lonely venture.** We need to teach them how to look up valid information, how to decipher between good information and bad information, and how to use the information appropriately. The upcoming generations will have some big world problems to work through, and to do so, they will need to know how to find useful information and how to use it.

As the world has become more accessible in this age of technology, these generations will also need to learn how to work together. United they stand, divided they fall. And this story isn't a new one. Almost any game changer can tell you that they couldn't make big changes without support. The world will need to unite in order to solve long-standing problems. I'm talking about climate change, poverty, drug epidemics, hunger, the threat of nuclear war. These problems have existed for as long as anyone alive can remember and I'm not implying that this future generation will need to solve all of these problems, but I'm saying that there's a better chance of solving these together. It will take a world-wide effort.

Finally, and last but not least, teachers need to inspire through **EXPERIENCE**. By this I mean that any child can Google Shakespeare and have all of the facts of his life, death, and know the names of his masterpieces. This, however, doesn't mean that the child will know what love felt like to Romeo and Juliet. We can talk about poetry, but a student needs to be impacted by at least one poem in their lives to want to read poetry. A student needs to *experience* happiness, joy, pain, or empathy when reading words across a line in order to want to continue to write or read words across a line. I can look up the names and stories of operas, but until I'm seated feeling the vibrations throughout my body as the soprano sings, I can't understand why people listen to operas. We need to move into experiential learning because that is what we remember and how our minds are wired to truly imprint information.

Yes, knowledge is at our fingertips like never before, but what we do with that knowledge has to come from the heart. It has to come from a place of wonder. Our heart strings need to feel, or pulse, and in order to do that we need to help these children connect to the magnanimity of human achievement, by experiencing it.

# How To Be A Good Parent for A Teacher

There seems to be an imbalance at my school when it comes to parental involvement. There are highly involved parents, and then parents that you're lucky to see once a year. The disparity is huge. The effects on teachers, as a result, is also huge. And my intuition tells me that this probably happens at most schools.

On the one hand, you have teachers that have a class full of parents that are very aware of grades and very opinionated about how the classroom should run. Under normal circumstances, one or two of these sets of parents is a good thing because they'll volunteer to help the classroom any which way, and offer their time, money, and two cents. While these parents may be demanding when it comes to their child, it's manageable because it's only a few sets of them.

What happens, however, when the number of demanding parents becomes the majority of the classroom? Now, the teacher often feels like she or he is "walking on eggshells." Every decision for the classroom needs to be carefully analyzed and weighed. How will this impact the parents? Will I get too many complaints? If I don't do it, will I get too many complaints? What problems can I foresee if I do this? In this case, the classroom becomes limited because the teacher feels limited.

How can highly involved parents, instead, help a teacher out? First, they can become involved in helping the teacher with whatever the teacher needs for the classroom. Second, it will also help if parents remember that they are NOT the only parents, and keep concerns to a minimum.

Remember, most classrooms average about 20 students, which means that there are 40 parents. Not all 40 parents may be involved, but often there are two separate homes for a child, which requires some extra work in addressing the parents. Please, also remember, that there shouldn't be an expectation, as a parent, that if you volunteer or help out, that it will qualify your child for special treatment. This is a turn-off for teachers. Last but not least, a form of respect for teachers, or for anyone for that matter, is to always deal directly with the person if there is an issue or problem. If you have an issue/concern/problem with the teacher, please come to the teacher *first*. The teacher should respond by respecting the concern and taking action within a reasonable timeframe. If none is taken within a reasonable amount of time, then the parent has the right to speak about it with administration. It's very difficult to run a good classroom these days, and when a teacher feels unappreciated, or worse, attacked, then the feeling of "walking on eggshells" takes over and a teacher feels very limited. And please remember that, as with most things involving children, the ones who suffer the most are the children. If a teacher feels limited or attacked in her or his classroom, the children will feel that limitation or hesitancy in the classroom as well.

And now what about those parents that you wish you saw more than once a year? They are probably not the ones reading this book. In these cases, as a teacher, sometimes you wonder how these children make it to school and back because you never see the parents, hear from the parents, or see any measure of care from the parents. These children usually don't have all of their basic needs met, don't have any parental support at home, and will take forever to return a signed form. You wonder why they didn't bring a sweater to school when it's 20 degrees colder than usual. You wonder why they don't know if they have asthma when clearly they do. You wonder why you never get any requests from the parents, even when you send home report after report showing that their child is failing at Reading or Math, or both. You can't count on these parents to do anything extra, to help you with anything in the classroom, and often, you can't even count on them to discipline their child at home.

"Which parent is "better" for a teacher, you ask?" Neither. If you have the kindly-named "helicopter parents," then you can expect daily conferences, and having to explain every decision you make in the classroom to parents and administration. If you have the "nonexistent parents," then you can't count on any assistance at home, at school, and you cross your fingers that they'll pick up the phone, should you ever need to call them for something important. These parents infuriate you because you just don't feel that they care. Often times, you feel that the child is somewhat abandoned or neglected. There are usually behavior problems that go with it. Medication. Sometimes a lack of medication. Sometimes you have the grace of a social worker that knocks on your door once per week. Sometimes not.

What is the answer? *Balance*. Be a balanced parent. This means that you develop a relationship with the teacher as the year progresses, without being overbearing. As a parent, you should be aware of your child's grades and progress throughout the year, and request an average of a few meetings per year to discuss your child. Keep an eye out for what the classroom needs and make sure that the teacher knows that she or he can request your support, if you're able to give it, of course.

What about those parents that are *in absentia*? We can't change them, but we can reach out to them and try to make sure that they are informed. As parents that care, that are reading this book, be aware of the imbalances of most classrooms, and just do your best to balance out the scales for the teacher. It will be noticed and appreciated, I promise. And thank you.

A lot of people say to me that we should study Canada and Scandinavia because their education is better. They ask me why we can't adopt some of their ideas or systems.

While I do believe we should study other countries that do better with education, it's important to remember that we can't compare our population of over 300 million to that of 7 or 8 million. It's almost impossible to adopt certain standards just due to our size.

There is a vastness of diversity within the vast borders of the United States of America. Each state is almost as large as, or larger than some of the smaller countries of the world. And each location has its unique requirements and capabilities. [cxvi]

# A NEW MODEL

Being present to the times in which we're living, it's clear that education must evolve in order to be successful. Even if your knowledge about public education is very limited, you can probably agree that the system is in need of reform. The following are my thoughts for a new model of education:

*Big, big ideas*

**A-political Money**

Can we figure out a route where local tax money can go directly to the district, and stay there, for education purposes? Presently, the state collects all local monies and then re-distributes them, which usually causes major disparities between districts. Or some districts become "donor" districts, which means that they support other districts that have less money, but usually the "donor" is a bigger district with greater needs that can't afford to donate money. I want voters and parents to realize that the property taxes they're paying to the state is re-routed a million times and the actual benefit their child is directly receiving for education purposes is not much. Superintendent Alberto Carvalho, of Miami-Dade County Public Schools, recently figured out how to raise money locally for the purpose of increasing teacher salaries and hiring security at schools through Referendum 362. This referendum has raised $232 million per year for the next four years, and it's only costing homeowners about $12 a month. How can we do this on a grand scale? How can we bypass politicians and place tax dollars directly in the hands of educators hired to run a district? IT'S YOUR MONEY. I'm just asking the questions.

**A New School Board**

Who should we put in charge of making big decisions about curriculum and the ins and outs of local schools? Most people would agree that trying to regulate schools nationally or via state is probably a mistake. There are too many differences amongst regions and localities to have a one-size-fits-all model for schools. In the place of national and state governments then, who gets to decide school design? In my opinion, it should be impartial, apolitical, teachers with at least 10 year of experience. Why 10 years? Because that means that they were serious about their teaching career and amassed enough experience to truly know what they're talking about when it comes to teaching. Should these teachers be elected? Probably. Should there be term limits? Yes. As times change, and cycles continue, there always needs to be fresh perspectives to keep up with the evolution of education.

## *Ideas FOR Teachers*

### **Specials Teachers –Art, Spanish, Music, PE**

What is a *specials* teacher? They are teachers that gift your child with fine arts, motor skills, and foreign languages. They are different from the general education teacher and don't usually have classroom obligations. Presently, *specials* teachers are a rare bird. First of all, it's difficult to get this position as there aren't a lot of positions open. As most schools are down to one teacher for each of these subjects, thanks to budget cuts, it's almost impossible to find a job in these non-core subjects since most *specials* teachers will try to stay at their school indefinitely –or at least until retirement. As a result, there's a disincentive to even *become* a teacher for these subjects because it will be that much harder for you to get a job!

*Specials* teachers have a very different schedule than a regular classroom teacher. Most of the time, they don't have a classroom and, therefore, are not subjected to extra classroom duties such as cleaning, decorating, dispensing/collecting paperwork, parent communication/conferences, or planning for events in the classroom. Through no fault of their own, *specials* teachers may feel resentment from regular classroom teachers due to this "lack" of extra duties. In addition, *specials* teachers sometimes have a lot more planning time or "time off" than a regular classroom teacher does –and they get paid the same amount! This fact adds to the resentment factor emanating from the classroom teachers, which is understandable as well, since most classroom teachers are overwhelmed most of the time.

How do we fix this inequity amongst teachers? First of all, let's acknowledge the fact that children *need* music, art, foreign languages, and physical education in their lives. Let's acknowledge the importance of these subjects and the talented people who teach them. Second, let's balance the scales. In order to solve most of our problems in the school setting, we need to think with unity. There needs to be "a highest good for all" mentality in order for a school to run well. For this reason, *specials* teachers should do other necessary tasks during their "extra hours" in order to create harmony. A good administrator will use the talents and skills of *specials* teachers wisely and fairly, thereby reducing inequalities and resentment amongst teachers.

## *30 Years*

Is this the ideal number for a teacher? 30 years. Well, that is what the state of Florida has decided it needs to be. Other states may require 25 years, and even this varies given the myriad of possibilities when it comes to retirement and pension plans.[cxvii] There's no question that teaching is like a fine wine. It takes time to become an expert at anything and teaching is no exception. Every year tacks on invaluable experience and that is what counts and becomes most valuable, like in any other profession. A teacher should be considered highly valuable, or indispensable, after 10 years or more. The school system should be focused on making sure that a teacher stays after so much time and investment. The system, which includes parents, should be committed to making sure that every teacher reaches this milestone because it's in the best interest of the world at large. In order for a teacher to stay for this long, however, things will have to change from how they presently are. At the present rates of teacher dropout, the percentage of teachers that will actually make it to 30 years is very low. And, if you ask any teacher that is presently close to this 30-year mark, she or he will tell you that the only reason they've made it this far is because teaching wasn't as difficult when they started, back 20 or 25 years ago. I have been told by a few of these veteran teachers that they wouldn't have "made it" if the system had been as difficult when they first began. Is teaching a profession that should be capped sooner because of its difficulty level, or do we just need to vastly improve conditions in order to require 30 years?

## *Opt Years*

What happens to a teacher after so many years of opening up a school year and closing it down? A teacher often gets burned out. The heavy lifting required from a tedious beginning and a hectic ending is very tiresome. It becomes common for a teacher to feel big negative effects after approximately ten years. Teachers who fall out of the system always comment, "it's just so hard to be a teacher. It takes so much work." I've heard this from many intelligent, highly motivated, very active teachers who could excel at many other professions. A new possibility for teachers in the system would be to have an "opt year." This means that teachers would take on another position approximately every five years. This would provide a break from the routine, and from the very challenging academic year with the children. The purpose of these opt years is to prevent teacher burnout if we desire teachers to be in the system for at least 30 years. Therefore, every five years or so, a teacher will have the option to serve for one academic year in another capacity. For example, it can be administrative work within the same school, at another school, or higher up at the district levels. In this way, the teacher would learn new skills, she or he would be able to be in a new environment, and she or he would take on a different perspective within the school system that would likely add to her or his professional growth. In return, the community would get a classroom teacher with a renewed spirit. In this way, the teacher is constantly growing professionally, which is important for her or his skills and spirit. It's a win-win: the children will be exposed to a happier and more productive professional, and the school system will continue to get its work done by simply swapping professionals and skills. There's logistics that need to be worked out, but what's possible? How can we think outside the box?

## *Ideas for Students*

### **Class size**

There's a reason that there are laws limiting class sizes. In order for one teacher to give 100% to all of her or his students, the number of students needs to be limited. Teachers are human. Education has shifted from the traditional model of rows with a teacher lecturing from the front of the class to desks put together in small groups, with children collaborating and speaking often. We now encourage teamwork in order for children to learn from each other, and center work which allows for a teacher to address the lessons of the day in a small group. Small groups are important because a teacher can ensure that every child in that small group is paying attention and is understanding. In addition, this opens up the classroom to collaborative learning. If one student can teach another student a skill, then you know that child has truly mastered the skill. Smaller class sizes need to be universally adopted and enforced in order to get the best results for each child.

### **School Calendar/Time**

Other large, industrialized countries like China, South Korea, Japan or Australia, teach year-round and have sizeable breaks every few months, without having one very long break like our summer break here in the United States. The problem with a long break is that students forget a lot over the summer and the routine is heavily disrupted. It would be better to consider eliminating it and having two to three week breaks every few months. This will also allow for teachers to have a more equitable academic year with better spacing between breaks, and slow down the hyper-pace of a teacher. Another possibility is making the school day longer, but providing more breaks for the students throughout the day. As teachers, we all know what the "glazed" eyes mean for a student: the moment you realize that you could have a unicorn on your head and it won't matter. The student is saturated and isn't processing what you're saying anymore. We all have limitations and children are no exception. The attention span of young children is limited. Ask a scientist or psychologist and they'll tell you exactly how many minutes the attention span of a child, teenager, or adult *should be*. We need to ask ourselves, "how does a young child best learn?" The answer is in "small bites," which may require a longer school day.

## Bottom Line

It takes a lot of work to have a school run well, be consistent, and obtain results. There isn't any reason that the workforce employed at a school can't divide up the work better. Every school should be allowed to assess its manpower and delegate accordingly. The details must be revamped in order to better balance the system and better balance the workload. It would open up more employment opportunities for those seeking work in education, and more importantly, it would create better results for our children.

# Interviews With Teachers

## *Question: If there was one thing that you could change in the education system, what would it be?*

As I wrote this book, I started to think that it would be interesting to get the opinions of other teachers. After all, it's rare that I get to ask them what they think is missing or what we get to add to education. And so I went around my school, door-to-door, and started asking this one question. I received some great responses which I have included here. The greatest lesson I learned from this questioning is that teachers have the answers. They know how things can improve, what education needs, what their classrooms need. Education should be run by teachers. The teachers should be the decision-makers. I think if we adopted and committed to just a few of these ideas with fidelity, education would be a different story...a much more pleasant story to tell. Here are some of their ideas...

Answer: CURRICULUM

"There's no room for personalization of the content in the current curriculum. The teachers are uninspired and therefore the children are uninspired. The best and the worst part about teaching art is that I have no textbook and no assigned curriculum. I just have standards that I have to teach, but it's totally up to me how I choose to teach them. This puts a lot of pressure on me because I'm constantly having to create new lesson plans, but at the same time, it allows me to go to a museum and see a great exhibition and be inspired by that and create content based off of that. It keeps me on my toes in a great way and the children relate to that well."

-**Mrs. Silver**, *Art teacher*

Answer: HIERARCHY

"I would change the working culture at school. I would get rid of the idea of Mr. and Mrs. or so and so. I think we're all colleagues. I don't see anything wrong with speaking to administration on a first name basis. Formality. True leadership is about sharing roles and I've seen that in the districts when that idea of hierarchy is taken away, then there is a sense of belonging. When the teachers have a sense of belonging then there's a greater trickle down to the students. I'm not saying that students should lose this sense of formality and respect to their teachers. This sense of hierarchy creates a culture of being patronized, which I disagree with. I think that the role of administration is to facilitate, to provide resources, without intimidation and without this idea that I have a position that you don't have.

Teachers are being held accountable, but administrators aren't being held accountable for the way that they manage people. When there are issues between the staff and administrators, the district doesn't do anything about it. There's a recycled group of people that are mediocre in admin and there's no sense of accountability. A lot of these administrators are overworked too, but a lot of them don't have administrative capacities whatsoever. They have no sense of empowerment or even managing people. A lot of the things that happen in a school system would never happen in a private company. From disrespect towards colleagues to hierarchical processes, to the way people talk to each other sometimes, and the way that expectations are set.

I think if we can address the structure in schools from an administrative point of view then education would change drastically. I also think that the districts are getting too big. Miami-Dade County is too big. There's too much red tape, hierarchical and egocentric issues going on. I think schools should decide locally, in the community, what things need to be done to address their own population. We are the 4th largest district and we've surpassed Chicago recently by about 30-40,000 children, which might put us as the 3rd largest soon.

When the districts get this big, then there's no time to actually ask teachers what they need or find out what resources they're lacking. As an example, teacher observations are being done just to fulfill a checklist. At the end of the day, if the teachers don't do well, then the school doesn't do well."

**-Mr. Morris**, *IB Coordinator*

Answer: MENTAL HEALTH SUPPORT

"There should be at least three or four social workers on site just to meet the needs of every child and really being able to evaluate children. Home visits should be incorporated and I'd like to stress 'non-judgmental' home visits. We should be able to help parents out with parenting and we can come into the home from a non-judgmental place and that way the parents will be comfortable receiving aid as opposed to really waiting for things to get out of hand. You want to avoid a situation where Department of Children & Families has to come into a home because that's not coming from a non-judgmental place. Regular home visits in a school environment will be very helpful to the mental health of all children and parents."

**-Mr. Gabriel**, *Social Worker*

Answer: TEACHER : STUDENT RATIO

"The ratio of teacher to student, counselor to student needs to improve. There's a million holes in the system, but we can't really fix those holes until we can manage the population effectively. There's supposed to be one counselor to two hundred fifty kids and here there's one counselor to 'five hundred and something' kids which leads to why we have so many kids with socio, emotional issues that aren't addressed."

**-Ms. Fremson**, *Counselor*

Answer: READING INSTRUCTION

"I would change the way Reading is taught in schools. Children would get what they need. The children who have trouble reading need to have phonics until they learn to read. And the children, at the beginning, that are learning to read, need to have a system where they learn phonics on a day-to-day basis with skills that build upon each other. They need to read decodable books until they learn to read. Then they can read anything. Once they have a solid foundation in reading, they'll be able to have comprehension.

Second, character education is lacking. Kids come without knowing how to behave towards each other, or how to be kind to each other. They get angry; they don't know how to manage their anger. They hit. They lash out. And they need to learn how to behave and it's not happening at home. Now they need to learn this at school."

**-Mrs. Prieto**, *former Reading Coach*
*veteran 2$^{nd}$ grade teacher for 40 years*

Answer: PARENTAL ENGAGEMENT

"I think what's missing is more parental involvement. A lot of parents aren't really investing in their child's education and there's a lack of motivation and a lack of empowerment for the student. As a result, this trickles into their academics. They really don't put in effort, which makes the job for the teacher that much harder because they spend more time disciplining than teaching. It ultimately leads to teachers being exhausted and emotionally drained. They feel like they're driving this ship alone. I really believe in the concept of it taking a village to raise a child. If each system, starting with the family system, doesn't put in their input to really have a strong foundation for this child going into school, it makes it that much more difficult for the child to succeed academically, emotionally, psychologically, and intellectually as well."

-**Ms. Becca**, *Social Worker*

Answer: LEADERSHIP

"What I really want is for the powers above, the decision-makers, to put in place administrators, or people that make decisions that have integrity, care for children, all the strengths that make a person valuable to society. Otherwise the decisions that are made, if they aren't based on student interests and the world as a whole, will make children suffer and teachers suffer."

-**Mrs. Mitrani**, *Media Specialist*

Answer: TEACHER AIDES

"I would like more support for the children, especially for those that are falling behind. All teachers need an aid or another teacher that can come in and help with small groups, in order to assist the children in reaching their potential and the levels they should be reaching. We, the classroom teachers, don't have the time or resources to move these children forward, and we only end up focusing on the ones that can move quickly and easily without any additional help. These other children fall through the cracks because we don't have the time or the energy or resources to help them. It's a disservice to them."

-**Ms. Portella**, *5$^{th}$ grade veteran teacher*

Answer: EDUCATOR INDEPENDENCE

"I would change the rigid structure of the curriculum and the rigidity around how a teacher does things. I would prefer it if there wasn't a set way of doing things. The curriculum is important, of course, but we shouldn't have to follow such strict guidelines. Every year, we are introduced to a new group of children with different needs. Some children need more social skills. Some need more emotional skills. It's almost impossible for a teacher to address these very important needs of a child because the schedule that we have to follow doesn't allow for it. And, oftentimes, a child can't progress academically until those other needs are met. I wish that we could really address their needs. I wish that teachers had free reign to do what we think is best to support our children academically, emotionally, and socially."

**-Mrs. Carballosa**, *5th grade gifted teacher*

Answer: LESS IS MORE

"I would change the curriculum – the way it's structured. We teach too much in too little time and we don't go in-depth. Instead, we should teach less per grade level and go more in-depth. For example, in kindergarten, children should learn phonics, decoding, fluency, and handwriting skills. For math, in kindergarten, I would only teach two concepts: adding and subtracting. I would ensure that every child understands the concepts inside and out, backwards and forwards. As the child moves up every grade level, I would add new concepts to that solid foundation rather than just keep spiraling and repeating old concepts. It's really about less is more and allowing for mastery of the basics."

**-Mrs. Arsenault**, *3rd grade gifted teacher*

Answer: REPORT CARDS

"We need to change the way that we report on students: meaning report cards. The fact that students today get the same report cards that we, teachers, got when we were in elementary school is insufficient. It needs to evolve. We need to take into account more than "A1A" –which stands for the academic, effort, and conduct grades. There should be elements of the characteristics that are linked to success, according to research. Things like grit, perseverance, empathy, and communication skills. The soft skills so to speak. The things that can't be measured by a standardized test. I think schools need to do a better job at being sources of instruction in those areas, and also give feedback to parents. Through the IB program, we were doing that with the Learner Profile. I've dabbled with the thought of getting rid of grades, altogether, to truly bring out the best in each student. I don't know if there's enough benefit that comes from grades and a report card, in order to outweigh the harm that it does on a lot of students, especially when it comes to self-esteem and identity."

-**Mrs. Clark**, *veteran teacher and IB coordinator*

Answer: CURRICULUM

"I can't choose just one. Class sizes, more funding, and more money for resources are just a few. Academically speaking, I would focus on vertical alignment. I would change it to where the gaps weren't so big between each grade level. I would change *Common Core*. Mental health is a huge issue. Academically, I don't feel like we're serving these students correctly. I would change the curriculum, as well. In the south, I feel like we're not giving them what they need to be competitive against other states and other countries. I feel that the northeast does a better job with the curriculum. Our curriculum HAS to change."

-**Ms. Bressett**, *3rd grade teacher*

# PART VII
# IN GRATITUDE

## *An Ode to Teachers*

Teachers that are truly in this game do this job out of love, and because they love, and because they get to feel the love in return. I'm talking about good teachers who are truly invested in their craft. As in any other profession, there are examples of people doing something temporarily, or who haven't found their niche. I'm talking about a teacher that is doing it for the right reasons. This educator will gravitate towards enhancing the life of her or his students and their life as a whole little person. I'm not just talking about academics. I'm talking about the emotional and physical life, and the environment of each student. Because it's all a web that can't be separated and teachers see that and understand that you can't separate it. You can't partition a child's life and compartmentalize it any more than you can do that for an adult. Life doesn't work that way. It all has stepping stones, effects, consequences, ripples, and it all empties out onto one major ocean.

A child recognizes the love that a teacher gives. A child loves unconditionally in return. And a child is forever marked by a good teacher. Just ask anyone you know. Do they remember their good teachers? By name? By grade? What do they remember about them? Is it a coincidence that they remember them during such a formative time in their life? No. You can't fake it for children. They're too authentic and they recognize authenticity. They will call you out on it. If it's fake, they won't respond or they won't remember you. But if there's love –real love –they will feel it, hold it, and remember it forever. And that is why teachers who are really in this game do what they do.

Teachers need to be acknowledged for the selfless acts they accomplish day after day. They need to be acknowledged for the infinite acts of patience they display, for the tiresome pace that they keep throughout the school year, for the constant shower of love that they give to each of their students. They need to be acknowledged for the safe haven they create for so many less fortunate children.

They need to be acknowledged for the love of learning that they embody because it lights them up when they see a student understand something, or learn something. They get value or emotional reward when their students are progressing, growing, and reaching. Good teachers feel accomplishment when they're able to impart their knowledge, skills, and dreams to these young souls. Teachers feel reward, love, and accomplishment when in service to these children. Teachers are in service and of service.

Teaching is meant to be a noble profession. Teachers hold power. According to Malcolm Gladwell, a Canadian journalist, author and speaker, a teacher is a "gatekeeper" because if a teacher takes interest in a child, then that child will thrive. A teacher can break through demarcated lines of race, inequality, and discrimination.

What we battle at this moment in history is a system in the richest country of the world whereby the balance has been tipped over for a teacher. The weight has become too heavy and it seems that a teacher wears an anchor over her or his neck in most places around the country. With so many demands in the classroom, so many demands from the system, and so many demands from society, a teacher's job has become heavy, overbearing, and insatiable. The joy is stripped away.

# ACKNOWLEDGMENTS

First and foremost, to my editor, Ana Mantica. As fate would have it, I met Ana in Kindergarten and she quickly became my best friend. We shared teachers, books, sleepovers, and much of our childhood. We lost touch in our adolescence and young adulthood, and then as fate would have it, we crossed paths again as adult women. Ana has been the singular force behind the creation of this book. It wouldn't have been possible without her and I'm forever grateful. I honor and acknowledge her commitment, love, support, rigor, and excellence in every aspect of her life.

To my soul tribe: Marianna, Alicia, Mario, Martina, Willie, Jill, Christina, Elisa, Diana, Mykola, Ugo, Karan, Alain, Scott, Charlie, Rosie, Natalia, and Roxane. I couldn't have asked for better souls to walk this journey home. Thank you for your support with the book and, most importantly, for nourishing my soul day in and day out!

To the Post-it Tribe: Our dreams are for the taking! We get to dream together and then love and support one another to its manifestation. What a gift!

To my teacher friends and colleagues at South Pointe Elementary: I wrote this book as much for you as for me. I honor the love, commitment, and heart that you've put in all of these years for the children.

To my book supporters: Without your donations, this book wouldn't have been published as quickly, nor as professionally, as it was finished. My heart has overflowed with love and gratitude.

To the Gratitude community: You are committed to being the 2% of this world. You are leaders, visionaries, and brave ninjas living your lives to its utmost fullest and inspiring the rest of the world to do the same. You are my power posse. I am because you are. And I'm proud to call ML27FLL my team for life! Thank you for reminding me of who I am. I hope I can always do the same for you.

To the South Pointe Elementary community: Thank you for all of the love, support, trust, and beauty in this community. I have never encountered as many intelligent, giving, respectful, and appreciative teachers and parents in such a small place. A piece of my heart will always live there.

To my family: Dad, Mom, Alex, Fannie, and Vegas. You are my everything. You are my reason for so many things. Thank you to my brothers, who love me, and have all encouraged me to chase after my dreams, including from the other side. To my extensive extended family…thank you for the authentic love you always give me!

To my soul sister from another mother, Marianna. I wouldn't have finished this book in excellence and with such peace without your support. I am eternally grateful. I will repay you by walking home with you by your side.

To Lynn, my literary producer, who arrived on the scene in the perfect moment. Thank you for seeing this book, for seeing me, and for taking the reins. I couldn't have put this book in better hands. I honor you, and your expertise, and I'm happy to call you a friend.

To the multitude of teachers, mentors, acquaintances, strangers, and passersby on the street who gave me a word of encouragement, a viewpoint, or a pat on the back, I thank you! I know you were placed there for a purpose, and I honor such a Divine Plan.

My pen is my sword. I do it because it's a part of my life's purpose and I'm happy it chose me.

# How This Book Came to Be

I felt that I had so much to say. I had observed so much, asked myself so many questions, asked others so many questions about the way things are, were, and operated. I kept thinking to myself, "I should write a book. I can write a book about all of this because people deserve to know. The citizens that pay for public education have a right to know about what goes on, how it goes on, and why. Or at least ask themselves 'why?' because a straight answer may not be in the cards."

After I started on a journey of transformational trainings, I gained the confidence that I needed to write this book. I kept thinking to myself that I had such a unique perspective that people would want to listen to me. People would care about what I had in mind, or how I saw things. After all, I'm a highly educated individual that went to parochial private schools, but has solely taught in public schools. Unique. I know the way things can be run coming from private schools and universities, and then compare that to the way things are run in public education. Shell-shock.

I also have a legal background. I went to the University of Pennsylvania Law School. I learned about how our system and government is set up and have some background on the division of power in this country. I started to ask big questions because I have enough knowledge to ask the question, WHY IS IT DONE THIS WAY or WHY ISN'T IT DONE THIS WAY?

As I continued to reflect, I realized that my perspective was indeed unique. And as I reflected on it more, I thought to myself that it was probably very unique -a perspective of one. How many people do you know that went to an Ivy League law school and then wound up as an elementary public school teacher? None. The first question that I usually get, is WHY???????

The answer to that question is both sad and inspirational at the same time. After graduating from law school in 2007, I found myself engulfed in personal family responsibility and desperate for a job.

For whatever reason, getting a job after my second year of law school became inexplicably difficult. When I returned (reluctantly) to Miami, I took the Florida Bar exam and didn't pass. Something inside of me told me that I had needed one more week to be ready for it. Failing the bar for the first time is a BIG deal because your likelihood of passing it afterward drops significantly. It's a very psychological test.

I pursued the bar exam three more times. I gave it my all. I studied on my own focusing on my weaknesses during the test, I acquired the help of a friend who helped coach me through my weaknesses, and eliminated all of the factors that I felt had set me up for failure the first time. I still failed it by six points.

There was no rhyme or reason for my not passing. I didn't have problems with tests growing up. They had been easy for me, as for most students who reach the hallways of the Ivy League. But whatever the reason was, it didn't matter. I had decided that if I didn't pass the fourth time around, I would walk away from it. Practicing law wasn't in the cards for me. I took it as a sign. I wanted a full-time job; a new career. I wanted to make money and live a normal life, as opposed to remaining a prisoner to the Bar.

But what would I do? What does a highly educated woman with a lot of student loan debt do to make a living? Who hires History majors with a *Juris Doctor* degree? WHO?

Restaurants. Restaurants don't discriminate. If you can take orders, bring food to a table, and do it with a smile on your face, you're hired! And that's how I started to make a living. In the meantime, I pondered what to do next. I kept hearing from friends, loved ones, and random strangers that I would make a good teacher. I should think about teaching. Then a good friend of mine told me about this movie that she found impactful. It was called, *Waiting for Superman*.

I found it at my local movie theater and went to see it. I was blown away by it. Something inside of me woke up. I felt inspired. Something told me that I should look into it. Soon thereafter, I decided to become a substitute teacher to see if the classroom could be a good fit for me. After all, I had never tried it. On the first day of walking into a new school to be a substitute teacher, I knew I had found something. My instincts kicked in and I knew I belonged. I knew I was a natural.

My journey as a substitute teacher lasted one year. I was able to gain experience at two schools in Miami Beach rather quickly. Before I knew it, I was offered a full-time position at South Pointe Elementary, where I continued my entire teaching career. For my first four years as a teacher, I was completely consumed by it. I lived it and breathed it. There was a moment for me where the full realization hit me that the learning curve was quite steep. I also had an intuitive knowing that this was the kind of profession where there was always more to learn. Always more to improve upon. With so many factors affecting your day-to-day or your school year, it is almost impossible to be completely comfortable with anything for very long in the school setting.

And so I dove in. I dove into acquiring knowledge, experience, asking questions, getting to know other teachers, reading books, taking professional development courses. I chose this as my profession with as much fervor as it had chosen me. Whenever a school break would come, I wouldn't know what to do with myself. It's the only time I would realize that I had a life outside of school that I was somewhat ignoring. Slowly but surely, I would "take my nose out of the book" to realize that there were other facets of my life that needed to be developed.

And so as the years went on and I acquired more knowledge, I started noticing things. I started wondering about how things worked and why. I started asking questions. And it didn't take long for me to realize that a lot of things didn't make sense to me. A lot of things didn't make sense to a lot of, *us*, teachers. And the reasons for having things be a certain way didn't seem to make a lot of sense to anyone, including to administration. I kept seeing money, time, resources, and energy wasted away. And the recurring theme continued to be, WHY? Why is this done this way? Isn't there a better way? Why should we waste time and energy on this?

And slowly but surely, this book began to write itself in my thoughts. This book began to come to life.

# ABOUT THE AUTHOR

Ingrid Laos was born and raised in Miami, Florida. As the daughter of Peruvian immigrants, her upbringing and perspective was always somewhat unique. She attended private, religious schools as a child and adolescent in Miami. She earned her Bachelor of Arts in History at the University of Miami and her Juris Doctor at the University of Pennsylvania Law School. She taught in the public school system in Miami Beach, Florida, for eight years. She lives and works serving children and parents in Miami.

# ENDNOTES

[i] Ridenour, Matt. "MATT RIDENOUR." *MATT RIDENOUR*, 3 Oct. 2013, mattridenour.net/.
[ii] Akadjian, David. "7 Things Our Founders Believed about Public Education." *Daily Kos*, 27 Jan. 2015, www.dailykos.com/.
[iii] Akadjian, David. "7 Things Our Founders Believed about Public Education." *Daily Kos*, 27 Jan. 2015, www.dailykos.com/.
[iv] "Superintendent of Schools –History, Importance in Education, New Expectations, An Evolving Role." *StateUniversity.com*, education.stateuniversity.com/.

[v] "Why Do States Have Rule Over Education?" *Nology.com*, www.teach-nology.com/.

[vi] "The Roles of Federal and State Governments in Education." *Findlaw*, education.findlaw.com/.

[vii] "Superintendent of Schools –History, Importance in Education, New Expectations, An Evolving Role." *StateUniversity.com*, education.stateuniversity.com/.

[viii] "How Are The Local, State And Federal Governments Involved in Education? Is This Involvement Just?" *Center for Public Justice*, cpjustice.org/public/page/content/homepage.

[ix] "Superintendent of Schools –History, Importance in Education, New Expectations, An Evolving Role." *StateUniversity.com*, education.stateuniversity.com/.

[x] "How to Become a Superintendent." *Teacher.org*, www.teacher.org/.

[xi] "Superintendent of Schools –History, Importance in Education, New Expectations, An Evolving Role." *StateUniversity.com*, education.stateuniversity.com/.

[xii] "Superintendent of Schools –History, Importance in Education, New Expectations, An Evolving Role." *StateUniversity.com*, education.stateuniversity.com/.

[xiii] "Superintendent of Schools –History, Importance in Education, New Expectations, An Evolving Role." *StateUniversity.com*, education.stateuniversity.com/.

[xiv] "Superintendent of Schools –History, Importance in Education, New Expectations, An Evolving Role." *StateUniversity.com*, education.stateuniversity.com/.

[xv] Litvinov, Amanda. "What If...Congress Kept Its Promises to Our Most Vulnerable Students?" *NeaToday*, Apr. 2019, pp. 14–15.

[xvi] Litvinov, Amanda. "What If...Congress Kept Its Promises to Our Most Vulnerable Students?" *NeaToday*, Apr. 2019, pp. 14–15.

[xvii] Muller, Jane. "The Governors' Role in Education: An Information Overview." *ERIC*, www.eric.ed.gov/.

[xviii] Litvinov, Amanda. "Midterm Elections Are Critical for Public Education." *NeaToday*, Oct. 2018, pp. 14–15.

[xix] "Superintendent of Schools- History, Importance in Education, New Expectations, An Evolving Role." *StateUniversity.com*, education.stateuniversity.com/.

[xx] Hornbeck, Dustin. "Federal Role in Education Has a Long History." *The Conversation*, 26 Apr. 2017, theconversation.com/.

[xxi] Klein, Alyson. "No Child Left Behind Overview." *Education Week*, 10 Apr. 2015, www.edweek.org/ew/index.html.

[xxii] "How Are The Local, State And Federal Governments Involved in Education? Is This Involvement Just?" *Center for Public Justice*, cpjustice.org/public/page/content/homepage.

[xxiii] Klein, Alyson. "The Every Student Succeeds Act: An ESSA Overview." *Education Week*, 31 Mar. 2016, www.edweek.org/ew/index.html.

[xxiv] Hornbeck, Dustin. "Federal Role in Education Has a Long History." *The Conversation*, 26 Apr. 2017, theconversation.com/.

[xxv] https://www.pea.com/airline-pilot-salary/

[xxvi] https://www.recruiter.com/salaries/heating-and-air-conditioning-mechanics-and-installers-salary/

[xxvii] https://www.allnursingschools.com/articles/nursing-salaries/

[xxviii] https://physicaltherapysalary.org

[xxix] https://money.usnews.com/careers/best-jobs/veterinarian/salary

[xxx] https://www.pharmacytimes.com/contributor/alex-barker-pharmd/2016/04/2016-pharmacist-salary-guide

[xxxi] https://money.usnews.com/careers/best-jobs/real-estate-agent

[xxxii] https://money.usnews.com/careers/best-jobs/accountant/salary

[xxxiii] https://www.payscale.com/research/US/Job=Stock_Broker/Salary

[xxxiv] https://www.glassdoor.com/Salaries/professor-salary-SRCH_KO0,9.htm

[xxxv] "First & Foremost: Who Is the Average Teacher?" *NeaToday*, Oct. 2018, pp. 10–13.

[xxxvi] Gabbatt, Adam, and Mike Elk. "Teachers' Strikes: Meet the Leaders of the Movement Marching across America ." *The Guardian*, Guardian News and Media, 16 Apr. 2018, https://www.theguardian.com/.

[xxxvii] "P.S.305."

[xxxviii] "Public Education in Florida." *Ballotpedia*, ballotpedia.org/Main_Page.

[xxxix] *Florida Governor Ron DeSantis*, http://www.flgov.com/.

[xl] Maciag, Mike. "The States That Spend the Most (and the Least) on Education." *Governing*, Aug. 2016, www.governing.com/.

[xli] Maciag, Mike. "The States That Spend the Most (and the Least) on Education." *Governing*, Aug. 2016, www.governing.com/.

[xlii] Maciag, Mike. "The States That Spend the Most (and the Least) on Education." *Governing*, Aug. 2016, www.governing.com/.

[xliii] Maciag, Mike. "The States That Spend the Most (and the Least) on Education." *Governing*, Aug. 2016, www.governing.com/.

[xliv] Maciag, Mike. "The States That Spend the Most (and the Least) on Education." *Governing*, Aug. 2016, www.governing.com/.

[xlv] Maciag, Mike. "The States That Spend the Most (and the Least) on Education." *Governing*, Aug. 2016, www.governing.com/.

[xlvi] Maciag, Mike. "The States That Spend the Most (and the Least) on Education." *Governing*, Aug. 2016, www.governing.com/.

[xlvii] "Charter Schools in Florida." *Ballotpedia*, https://ballotpedia.org/Main_Page.

[xlviii] McClellan, Amy. "All about Florida Charter Schools." *Home*, https://www.floridacharterschools.org/.

[xlix] Strauss, Valerie. "Florida's Charter-School Sector Is a Real Mess." *The Washington Post*, WP Company, 3 May 2019, https://www.washingtonpost.com/.

[l] "Public Education in Florida." *Ballotpedia*,

https://ballotpedia.org/Main_Page.

[li] Solodev. "Charter Schools." *Www.fldoe.org*, http://www.fldoe.org/.

[lii] Litvinov, Amanda, et al. "The DeVos Connection." *NeaToday*, Aug. 2018, pp. 14–15.

[liii] Alvarez, Brenda, et al. "Top 10 Challenges Facing Educators." *NeaToday*, Aug. 2018, pp. 36–43.

[liv] Travis, Scott. *Florida Charter Schools: Here's What Will Change under Education Overhaul*. 15 June 2017, sun-sentinel.com.

[lv] Travis, Scott. *Florida Charter Schools: Here's What Will Change under Education Overhaul*. 15 June 2017, sun-sentinel.com.

[lvi] Travis, Scott. *Florida Charter Schools: Here's What Will Change under Education Overhaul*. 15 June 2017, sun-sentinel.com.

[lvii] Travis, Scott. *Florida Charter Schools: Here's What Will Change under Education Overhaul*. 15 June 2017, sun-sentinel.com.

[lviii] Travis, Scott. *Florida Charter Schools: Here's What Will Change under Education Overhaul*. 15 June 2017, sun-sentinel.com.

[lix] Maxwell, Scott. "'Failing' Schools? Charter Schools Get F's Three Times as Often in Florida." *Orlandosentinel.com*, Orlando Sentinel, 29 June 2017, https://www.orlandosentinel.com/.

ix Travis, Scott. *Florida Charter Schools: Here's What Will Change under Education Overhaul.* 15 June 2017, sun-sentinel.com.

xi Travis, Scott. *Florida Charter Schools: Here's What Will Change under Education Overhaul.* 15 June 2017, sun-sentinel.com.

lxii Strauss, Valerie. "Florida's Charter-School Sector Is a Real Mess." *The Washington Post*, WP Company, 3 May 2019, https://www.washingtonpost.com/.

lxiii Strauss, Valerie. "Florida's Charter-School Sector Is a Real Mess." *The Washington Post*, WP Company, 3 May 2019, https://www.washingtonpost.com/.

lxiv Strauss, Valerie. "Florida's Charter-School Sector Is a Real Mess." *The Washington Post*, WP Company, 3 May 2019, https://www.washingtonpost.com/.

lxv Strauss, Valerie. "Florida's Charter-School Sector Is a Real Mess." *The Washington Post*, WP Company, 3 May 2019, https://www.washingtonpost.com/.

lxvi "State Laws." *Findlaw*, https://statelaws.findlaw.com/.

lxvii "New York Unions: What You Need to Know." *BLR® - Solutions for Employment, Safety and Environmental Compliance | BLR.com*, https://www.blr.com/.

[lxviii] DePillis, Lydia. "Here's What Happened to Teachers after Wisconsin Gutted Its Unions." *CNN*, Cable News Network, 17 Nov. 2017, https://www.cnn.com/BUSINESS.

[lxix] DePillis, Lydia. "Here's What Happened to Teachers after Wisconsin Gutted Its Unions." *CNN*, Cable News Network, 17 Nov. 2017, https://www.cnn.com/BUSINESS.

[lxx] Warner, Joel. "'We're Not Gonna Take It!': Can Trump Country Withstand the Grassroots Teachers Movement Sweeping the Nation?" *Newsweek*, 12 July 2018, https://www.newsweek.com/.

[lxxi] Hinrichs, Erin. "In Wake of Supreme Court Ruling on Union Fees, Minnesota Teachers Decide Whether to Opt out or Go All In." *MinnPost*, 12 July 2018, https://www.minnpost.com/.

[lxxii] Hinrichs, Erin. "In Wake of Supreme Court Ruling on Union Fees, Minnesota Teachers Decide Whether to Opt out or Go All In." *MinnPost*, 12 July 2018, https://www.minnpost.com/.

[lxxiii] "First & Foremost: Supreme Court Ruling Deals Blow to Working Families in 'Janus.'" *NeaToday*, Aug. 2018, pp. 10–13.

[lxxiv] Kamenetz, Anya, and Ari Shapiro. "Now It's North Carolina Teachers' Turn: How Did We Get Here? What's Next?" *NPR*, NPR, 15 May 2018, https://www.npr.org/.

[lxxv] Flannery, Mary Ellen, and Amanda Litvinov. "The Cost of Education Funding Cuts." *NeaToday*, Aug. 2018, pp. 31–32.

[lxxvi] Warner, Joel. "'We're Not Gonna Take It!': Can Trump Country

Withstand the Grassroots Teachers Movement Sweeping the Nation?" *Newsweek*, 12 July 2018, https://www.newsweek.com/.

lxxvii Flannery, Mary Ellen, and Amanda Litvinov. "Why We Are Red for Ed." *Education Votes*, https://educationvotes.nea.org/.

lxxviii Flannery, Mary Ellen. "Why We Are Red for Ed ." *NeaToday*, Oct. 2018, pp. 34–35.

lxxix Flannery, Mary Ellen, and Amanda Litvinov. "Why We Are Red for Ed." *Education Votes*, https://educationvotes.nea.org/.

lxxx Flannery, Mary Ellen, and Amanda Litvinov. "Why We Are Red for Ed." *Education Votes*, https://educationvotes.nea.org/.

lxxxi Flannery, Mary Ellen, and Amanda Litvinov. "The Cost of Education Funding Cuts." *NeaToday*, Aug. 2018, pp. 31–32.

lxxxii Flannery, Mary Ellen, and Amanda Litvinov. "Why We Are Red for Ed." *Education Votes*, https://educationvotes.nea.org/.

lxxxiii "North Carolina Teachers Will Be the next to Walk out. Here's What They Want." *CNN*, Cable News Network, 15 May 2018, http://news.blogs.cnn.com/tag/the-cnn-wire/.

lxxxiv "First & Foremost: UTLA Strike Leads to Historic Agreement." *NeaToday*, Apr. 2019, pp. 10–13.

lxxxv Litvinov, Amanda. "Your Year in Activism." *NeaToday*, June 2019, pp. 12–13.

[lxxxvi] Flannery, Mary Ellen. "Why We Are Red for Ed ." *NeaToday*, Oct. 2018, pp. 34–35.

[lxxxvii] Warner, Joel. "'We're Not Gonna Take It!': Can Trump Country Withstand the Grassroots Teachers Movement Sweeping the Nation?" *Newsweek*, 12 July 2018, https://www.newsweek.com/.

[lxxxviii] Warner, Joel. "'We're Not Gonna Take It!': Can Trump Country Withstand the Grassroots Teachers Movement Sweeping the Nation?" *Newsweek*, 12 July 2018, https://www.newsweek.com/.

[lxxxix] Reilly, Katie. "Most Teachers Running for Office Lost on Tuesday. Here's Why Educators Are Celebrating the 2018 Midterms Anyway." *Time*, Time, 9 Nov. 2018, https://time.com/.

[xc] Litvinov, Amanda. "Your Year in Activism." *NeaToday*, June 2019, pp. 12–13.

[xci] Warner, Joel. "'We're Not Gonna Take It!': Can Trump Country Withstand the Grassroots Teachers Movement Sweeping the Nation?" *Newsweek*, 12 July 2018, https://www.newsweek.com/.
[xcii] Warner, Joel. "'We're Not Gonna Take It!': Can Trump Country Withstand the Grassroots Teachers Movement Sweeping the Nation?" *Newsweek*, 12 July 2018, https://www.newsweek.com/.
[xciii] Warner, Joel. "'We're Not Gonna Take It!': Can Trump Country Withstand the Grassroots Teachers Movement Sweeping the Nation?" *Newsweek*, 12 July 2018, https://www.newsweek.com/.
[xciv] Warner, Joel. "'We're Not Gonna Take It!': Can Trump Country Withstand the Grassroots Teachers Movement Sweeping the Nation?" *Newsweek*, 12 July 2018, https://www.newsweek.com/.
[xcv] Warner, Joel. "'We're Not Gonna Take It!': Can Trump Country Withstand the Grassroots Teachers Movement Sweeping the Nation?" *Newsweek*, 12 July 2018, https://www.newsweek.com/.

[xcvi] "First & Foremost: A National Epidemic of Untrained Teachers." *NeaToday*, Jan. 2019, pp. 10–13.

[xcvii] Warner, Joel. "'We're Not Gonna Take It!': Can Trump Country Withstand the Grassroots Teachers Movement Sweeping the Nation?" *Newsweek*, 12 July 2018, https://www.newsweek.com/.

[xcviii] Kamenetz, Anya, and Ari Shapiro. "Now It's North Carolina Teachers' Turn: How Did We Get Here? What's Next?" *NPR*, NPR, 15 May 2018, https://www.npr.org/.

[xcix] Kamenetz, Anya, and Ari Shapiro. "Now It's North Carolina Teachers' Turn: How Did We Get Here? What's Next?" *NPR*, NPR, 15 May 2018, https://www.npr.org/.

[c] Gurney, Kyra. "Living in Miami on a Teacher's Salary? Good Luck Finding a Place You Can Afford ." *South Florida Breaking News, Sports & Crime*, 20 Apr. 2017, https://www.miamiherald.com/.

[ci] "First & Foremost: Where Do Teachers Get the Most Respect?" *NeaToday*, Apr. 2019, pp. 10–13.

[cii] flsenate.gov

[ciii] LaGrone, Katie. "New Bill Proposes Major Changes to Florida's Teacher Certification Process." *WFTS*, Mar. 2019, https://www.abcactionnews.com/.

[civ] Alvarez, Brenda, et al. "Top 10 Challenges Facing Educators." *NeaToday*, Aug. 2018, pp. 36–43.

[cv] Veiga, Christina. "Controversial Standardized Tests Debut in Florida Schools." *Miamiherald.com*, 1 Mar. 2015.

[cvi] https://dictionary.cambridge.org/us/
[cvii] "First & Foremost: Got Counselors?" *NeaToday*, June 2019, pp. 10–11.

[cviii] Walker, Tim. "Are Schools Prepared to Tackle the Mental Health Crisis?" *NeaToday*, Oct. 2018, pp. 44–47.

[cix] Alvarez, Brenda, et al. "Top 10 Challenges Facing Educators." *NeaToday*, Aug. 2018, pp. 36–43.

[cx] Walker, Tim. "Are Schools Prepared to Tackle the Mental Health Crisis?" *NeaToday*, Oct. 2018, pp. 44–47.

[cxi] Diaz, Amber. "Miami-Dade Spends $6.2 Million ." *Miami-Dade Spends $6.2 Million to Create Mental Health Department*, 17 Aug. 2018, miami.cbslocal.com/.
[cxii] Walker, Tim. "Are Schools Prepared to Tackle the Mental Health Crisis?" *NeaToday*, Oct. 2018, pp. 44–47.

[cxiii] "First & Foremost: On Gun Violence Educators Say No to Arming Teachers, Yes to Real Solutions." *NeaToday*, Aug. 2018, pp. 10–13.

[cxiv] Alvarez, Brenda, et al. "Top 10 Challenges Facing Educators." *NeaToday*, Aug. 2018, pp. 36–43.

[cxv] Strauss, Valerie. "Florida's Charter-School Sector Is a Real Mess." *The Washington Post*, WP Company, 3 May 2019, https://www.washingtonpost.com/.
[cxvi] "Why Do States Have Rule Over Education?" *Nology.com*,

www.teach-nology.com/.

[cxvii] Gassmann, Gabriel. "TeacherPensions.org." *TeacherPensions.org*, 12 July 2018, www.teacherpensions.org/.

# INDEX

## A

Academica, 40, 45, 46
accountability, 11, 12, 39, 136
administrators, 9, 26, 53, 63, 65, 88, 136, 139
anxiety, 100, 101

## B

Baker Act, 102
Betsy DeVos, 41
Broward County Public Schools, 35

## C

Charter schools, 39, 41
Class size, 37, 133, 141
Classroom teachers, 74
Congress, 9, 12, 13, 61, 155
Constitution, 3, 4, 5
counselor, 60, 99, 100, 137

## D

Democrats, 35, 61
depression, 100, 101

## E

Elementary and Secondary Education Act (ESEA), 12
Employee benefits, 37
Every Student Succeeds Act (ESSA), 13

## F

Federal law, 8
Florida legislature, 52, 56, 79

Framers, 3, 4, 5

## G

Google, 119, 120
governor, 9, 10, 13, 14, 35, 50, 57, 58, 87
Governor Rick Scott, 41, 42, 90
Governor Ron DeSantis, 157
gun, 105, 106

## H

Harmony Public Schools, 40

## I

IDEA, 9, 40

## K

KIPP, 40

## M

Mater charter, 46
medication, 93, 95, 125
meditation, 111, 112
Mental health, 141

## N

National Education Association (NEA), 105
National Heritage Academies, 40
No Child Left Behind Act (NCLB), 12

## P

Parkland, 101, 106

phonics, 138, 140
politicians, 10, 30, 49, 65, 87, 129
President Donald Trump, 13
psychologists, 94, 96, 100, 115
Public education, 79

## R

Referendum 362, 53, 129
retirement, 50, 63, 130, 131

## S

School boards, 57
security, 17, 45, 55, 129
shootings, 81, 101, 102, 105, 106
social workers, 94, 96, 99, 100, 115, 137
*Specials* teachers, 130

strike, 51, 57, 58, 59, 60
Superintendent, 6, 7, 8, 101, 129, 154, 155

## U

U.S. Supreme Court, 55
unions, 37, 49, 51, 52, 53, 54, 55, 57, 60, 61
United Teachers of Dade (UTD), 50

## V

value, iv, v, 22, 31, 82, 146

## Z

Zulueta brothers, 45

# THE DEATH OF PUBLIC SCHOOLS

# THE DEATH OF PUBLIC SCHOOLS

# THE DEATH OF PUBLIC SCHOOLS